VOICES FROM PEJUHUTAZIZI

VOICES
FROM
PEJUHUTAZIZI

DAKOTA STORIES AND STORYTELLERS

Teresa Peterson and Walter LaBatte Jr.

MINNESOTA
HISTORICAL
SOCIETY PRESS

The publication of this book was supported through a generous grant from the Elmer L. and Eleanor Andersen Publications Fund.

Unless otherwise credited, all historic photographs were provided by the authors and all contemporary photographs were taken by Karen Odden.

mnhspress.org

The Minnesota Historical Society Press is a member of the Association of University Presses.

Manufactured in the United States of America.

10 9 8 7 6 5 4 3

♾ The paper used in this publication meets the minimum requirements of the American National Standard for Information Sciences—Permanence for Printed Library Materials, ANSI Z39.48–1984.

International Standard Book Number
ISBN: 978-1-68134-184-2 (paperback)
ISBN: 978-1-68134-185-9 (e-book)

Library of Congress Control Number: 2021946451

This and other Minnesota Historical Society Press books are available from popular e-book vendors.

CONTENTS

PREFACE

••

Hau mitakuyapi. Greetings, my relatives.

When my grandfather Waŋbdiska died, almost all the adults among our extended family had the same lament: they wished they had written down all of Grandpa's stories. We did not know that Grandpa had, himself, recorded a number of them. In doing this, he preserved such knowledge for the next generations. So, by the same reasoning, I want to preserve the stories I heard in my youth from the elders of that era and to record my experiences of growing up on Pejuhutazizi. When I tell these stories, I am not speaking on behalf of anyone but myself and my family. These are the stories as I heard them and as I tell them. Other people may know different versions of these stories, and they're all good, all part of our community's cultural wealth.

I wonder if the elders of my youth ever noticed that I was listening and recording in my memory all the stories they told and wondered if I would become the storyteller of today. Those elders included my grandfather Waŋbdiska, all my aunts and uncles, Annie Adams, Eliza Cavender, Elizabeth Blue, Maude Ortley, and a host of others. None ever said, "Now remember this." It was all in an ordinary telling of seemingly little significance. I wonder, Who among the young of today is also listening, remembering, preparing to be the storyteller of tomorrow?

Ho hecetu, mitakuye owasiŋ.

Wašicuŋhdinaźiŋ—Walter "Super" LaBatte Jr.

INTRODUCTION

> *A people without the knowledge of their past history,*
> *origin and culture is like a tree without roots.*
> —MARCUS GARVEY

Francis tipped his cowboy hat back, looked at me, and said, "Your tree has no roots." I replied with silence and a blank stare. I looked down at my wispy, blowing-in-the-wind tree, drawn on the stark white eleven-by-fourteen-inch paper.

"You're searching for something," he declared.

This time I responded with a bewildered "What? What am I looking for?"

"That's for you to figure out," he replied.

And that was that. My *tree reading* was over. With nothing more to say, I shook his hand and thanked him. No epiphanies, no *Aha Oprah* moments. Thoughts briefly wafted through my mind on the drive home—I knew it was significant, but I was frustrated with my apparent lack of tree interpretation.

That was the spring of 2000. I was a wife and mother of two- and four-year-old boys, and I was working as a postsecondary counselor at a charter school serving predominantly Native students. We began our days with smudging, with the students circled around the drum singing the Dakota Flag Song. This cultural grounding happened before we moved into the academic routine. Our days were rooted in Dakota worldview, coupled with experiential learning and the traditional book learning. The small base of students and staff allowed us the flexibility to participate in community events, workshops, and conferences—those often filled by adults. It offered relevant and engaging educational experiences not often found in textbooks. We learned together, students and staff. One such community event included a two-day Red Road Gathering. During that second day of the workshop, with very little instruction, we were each asked to draw a tree. I had anxiously awaited my turn for a tree reading and wondered what someone could possibly glean from my dismally drawn and uninteresting tree.

I did not understand what any of this meant then, but it stuck with me over the years. It has taken me all this time to return to that place, now with more insight. I was, in essence, a tree with no roots. I grew up visiting my mother's family at the Upper Sioux Community, which we know as Pejuhutazizi K'api, the Place Where They Dig the Yellow Medicine. What I had understood and learned of my culture up to that point provided a foundation for my Dakota identity. And yet, in hindsight, I was missing so much. I once heard that knowing *who* you are has every bit to do with knowing *whose* you are. How does one come to understand who one belongs to? Dakota ia, Utuhu Caŋ Cistiŋna emakiyapi ye—*In Dakota, they call me Little Oak Tree.* I am the granddaughter of many... many of whom brought me here to this place in time.

I now realize it is stories that carry us from our past to our present and into our collective future. Many of the stories in this collection are of resiliency and strength, courage and fortitude. My ancestors' stories remind me that I am here not by chance, but for purpose. I am *meant* to be here. I have come to understand that we all have story. Our story shapes our sense of belonging and place in the world. When we know our story, we belong—no matter where we go, where we are.

Dakota Stories and Storytellers

Within our community, there are two types of stories. Wicooyake stories include history, migration, and genealogy of the people. Hituŋkakaŋpi stories include tales, legends, and myths. Both types of stories do more than entertain. They enlarge the mind and stimulate imagination. Hituŋkakaŋpi and wicooyake stories are sometimes kept alive through rare written accounts, yet some Dakota families and communities continue to rely upon the oral traditions of gifted storytellers.

The role of the storyteller is to preserve history and legend, pass on traditions and values, connect listeners to people and place, and entertain. Ella Deloria, a Dakota linguist, ethnographer, and author from the early 1900s, wrote of Dakota storytellers who could recall three hundred winter counts, all from memory and without error. Storytelling is a gift, and storytellers are loved and respected. The primary story-tellers in this collection are my great-grandpa Waŋbdiska, aka Fred Pearsall, and my uncle, dekši mitawa, Wašicuŋhdinažiŋ—aka Walter "Super" LaBatte Jr.

Waŋbdiska shares Dakota stories from long ago, including those he heard from his mother-in-law, Tašinasusbecawiŋ, my great-great-grandmother. Grandpa Fred—he was my great-grandfather, but I know him as Grandpa Fred—intended to publish his stories but did not live long enough to realize his goal. In 1983, his daughter Waŋske, aka Cerisse Pearsall Ingebritson, typed up and self-published a small edition of his stories as a book. She titled it *Short Stories and History of Dakota People (Sioux)* by Fred Pearsall, and she included sketches by her nephew Dean Blue. A reporter from the local newspaper inter-viewed her and reported that she "did it partly for those who still re-member her father... but the book holds much for those much younger as well." Mom gave me her copy when I left for college, and neither of us realized the importance of it at the time. It is long out of print, so my copy, now tattered and held together with a rubber band, is a treasured family heirloom.

In the 1990s, I was able to ask Cerisse about the book while visiting her sunny home in Phoenix. She was my grandma Genevieve's older sister—my great-aunt, but in the Dakota way, she would have just been my grandma. During these visits, I learned more about her and her sis-ters' early lives. She described how she and my grandma had to harness the horses to the wagon when they wanted to travel. She shared that she and Grandma were the first Indians to graduate from the public school in town, and she told me, "I don't know how Gen graduated because she never studied." While the sisters remained close, their demeanor and lifestyles seemed completely different. Cerisse lived a more prim and refined life, my grandma more common and comforting, much like my own mother. I appreciate both. Cerisse introduced me to new ideas, like Native art. She shared a story of having kept a friendship with R. C. Gorman, the famous Navajo painter, and she supported other artists with purchases of baskets, beadwork, and paintings. She encouraged me to pursue further education and a career, and I imagine that resonated with her own independent life. Eventually, we decided that I would rewrite her book so that others might enjoy her father's

Interviewing Great-Aunt Cerisse in the kitchen of her sunny home in Phoenix, 1990s.

stories. I am reminded of that promise as I walk from room to room in my home—an art card signed by Gorman and sent to Cerisse that hangs in my office, her baskets displayed in the living room, and a large oil painting from another artist hanging in my dining room. She died late in the summer of 2011, two weeks before her 101st birthday.

This collection joins the stories from Grandpa Fred contained in Cerisse's book with my uncle's stories. Dekśi Super, or Waśicuŋhdi-nażiŋ, shares his own memories and stories he heard growing up in Pejuhutazizi. From time to time, I heard Dekśi tell stories when he was giving a talk for a group, or at some formal presentation I had wheedled him into making. Sometimes, when I asked him for advice on some dilemma, he would tell me a story and expect me to figure out the solution on my own. On these occasions it might take me days to figure out what teaching the story had to offer. Recognizing his gift of stories and storytelling, I asked Dekśi to join me in completing this book project. With differing motivations, voices, and perspectives, we have had to figure out an amicable route for the book together. More importantly, we both agree stories are meant to be shared and passed from one generation to the next.

Coming Together

This project has taken detours, gotten lost, found new roads, and evolved into a broader collection of stories. *Voices from Pejuhutazizi: Dakota Stories and Storytellers* is organized into four parts. Part 1 answers the question "Why are these stories important to me?" Because I am the narrator, you will hear some of my stories from Pejuhutazizi: my own early experiences, and what happens when you learn the stories of your family and community.

Part 2 introduces the primary characters in the stories and traces the connections between them through four generations.

Part 3 is the collection of stories from Waŋbdiska and Wašicuŋhdi-nażiŋ. The stories are organized thematically, and they offer intersections across generations.

Stories impart values—teaching us how to live and behave from one generation to the next.

Stories transmit traditions—passing on cultural practices that give tribute and honor to unique ways of being and doing.

Stories deliver heroes—inspiring us through the actions of others, especially those we have not read about in school and can't find in history books.

Stories reconcile—offering understanding and opportunity to make things right.

Stories entertain—bringing delight to listeners.

Stories tell of place—reminding us of and connecting us to this land we call home.

Stories provide belonging—nurturing kinship, community, and connectedness.

As you read through the collection of stories, I encourage you to look for the teachings within each and their personal connections to your own story. This is the power of stories: they cultivate our shared humanity.

Part 4 answers the question "How have these stories changed me?"

I return to share how reclaiming stories strengthens my own sense of identity and belonging in the world.

While each voice is distinct, the storytellers are differentiated by type treatment. We include brief and limited annotation and a glossary with translations of Dakota words that are not defined in the text. As you read and connect with the storytellers and stories, you might recognize how in some ways we are all the same—and yet we are different. Perhaps you will be inspired to connect to your own family's and community's stories, because truly, we *all* have story.

PART 1. RETURNING THROUGH STORY

Utuhu Caŋ Cistiŋna / Teresa Peterson

One summer over the Fourth of July we took a visit to one of my husband's relatives in the Peever area, over on the Lake Traverse Reservation. This was a few years back, when our boys were young, and they loved running around with their tahaŋšis. It was the home of one of his "uncles," a relative of his grandma's that I had not yet met. After sharing a meal, visiting, and watching fireworks, we got up to head back to our motel, and I proceeded to shake everyone's hands. As I was going down the line of lawn chairs, I heard the uncle ask a younger relative next to him, "Who was that? See how she is. That's because she knows who she is." By that time in my life, I had learned enough of my family's story, gained enough confidence in my own identity, and I understood: when you know yourself, no matter where you go, you belong.

I have come to understand that stories are integral in shaping our cultural identities. Damakota—I am Dakota. It is through these stories I have a better understanding of what that means, what it means to be a Dakota wiŋyaŋ—a Dakota woman. I think a part of it is knowing who you are, who you belong to, and it is that understanding that is most often gained through stories. Sure, I was raised in relationship to my mother's family at the Upper Sioux Community: my grandma, my aunties and cousins, and all my extended relatives. But it was not until later in my life that I learned of our stories of long ago, our history told through story—stories of place, and stories of relatives and their resilience and strength. Stories of my great-great-grandmother whose life and legacy brought forward a daughter, five granddaughters, and ultimately me to this place and time that has become part of my story.

I am bicultural, Dakota and German. I grew up in an old farmhouse outside of St. Cloud, on land tucked in a country neighborhood void of any other Dakota people. I was not raised in my mother's homelands, with the comfort of Dakota relatives constantly nearby. To the contrary, mainstream society, the white society, enveloped me. It was everywhere in my childhood—school, media, neighbors, friends, and church. Yet

I inherently knew I was "Indian" and that I was different. But what did it mean to be "Indian" or "Sioux"? Other than my mom telling me to "marry Indian," I do not remember anyone explaining to me what that meant or sharing stories about our Dakota people or our ways.

Visiting my relatives and dancing at powwows with my cousins throughout my childhood likely contributed to some level of understanding. Maybe there was some biological knowing of place as my brother and I sat in the back seat of the car traveling south on Highway 23. *Are we there yet? When will we get there?* It would take our family less than three hours to get from the farm to my grandma and grandpa's home on the reservation. I felt emerging butterflies of excitement when we made the turn at the stop sign that showed we were three miles from Granite Falls before taking the right turn toward the big open river valley, who revealed herself as we drove down the winding hill.

It was somehow different from visits to my other grandma's—the German side of the family, in Gaylord. True, both places provided an extended loving family. At my grandma Meta's home, we were greeted

Me, at Upper Sioux powwow in 1973, down by the river.

with drawings of an Indian boy and girl displayed in their front window for all to see—perhaps a message to their neighbors or those passing by that they were Indian lovers. The drawings look kitschy now, but for me, they were a symbol of belonging, showing that I was welcome and loved. Yet going to my mom's side of the family was something special, like a place I was supposed to be. The reservation felt, ironically, free and liberating, with room to explore and be. Visits were typically during holidays, summers, or other extended times away from school. My cousins and I took turns begging my mom to let me stay beyond the usual day trip. She got irritated, but she most often gave in to our persistence.

I seemed to have a deeply rooted desire and pull to be in this place with my relatives at Pejuhutazizi. My childhood memories of fun-filled visits connect seasonal experiences to place and land. For example, in the winter, we climbed to the top of the hill where my cousins lived. Then we slid down the hill, past another aunt's house, and finally down to the giant oaks below my grandma and grandpa's place. We repeated this climb over and over, until we could not feel our fingers or one of us was injured. In fact, I hold scars and story to prove it. In the summer, my cousins and I rode horses up and down the deer and people trails, bringing them to the creek to quench their thirst—us girls with our feet kicked up along their manes, hoping they wouldn't roll us into the water. Hot summer days, we swam at the creek and dared each other to swim over beneath the culvert. Hiking to the river bottom, we climbed over giant felled cottonwoods to reach the Mni Sota Wakpa, where we sunned near shallow pebbled areas and kept a lookout for snakes. We pestered their mom—my summer mother—for candy sold at the tribal government building where she worked. We played hide-and-seek and kickball with the kids on the next hill over and were among many more taking turns running around the seated circle of Duck, Duck, Gray Duck in front of the community hall. We drank from the spring on the side road past one aunt's home to another. During powwow time, my cousins and I helped collect entrance dollars from white visitors and pointed to where the "secret" spring was. As long as we ate our egg-and-Spam sandwiches and were back by the evening, we could be feral children, exploring the hills and valleys along the Minnesota River. These liberating experiences with relatives that looked more like me than my Polish and German neighbors made me feel at home.

Grandpa and Grandma LaBatte in front of their house with my younger cousin and me, about 1972.

Unlike back home on the farm, where every day was a chore day, Saturdays at my cousins' were designated as the chore day. Perhaps this was a carryover from boarding school days, when Aŋpetu Owaŋkayuźaźa was named as floor-washing day. We washed and dried lots of laundry on the long clotheslines behind their home that overlooked the hillside. On Sundays we went to church, where I tried to make sense of the Dakota words spoken through Reverend Tang's Chinese accent and pretended to singsong along as relatives pointed to the correct pages in the *Dakota Odowaŋ*, the book of Dakota hymns. I remember hearing this "Indian" language also spoken in secret between my grandparents. It was as if they had something important to say that was not meant for us kids to know. This was my mother's own personal memory as well—that the language was relegated to her parents' generation. Thus, my mother did not learn or speak Indian (as we said), and neither did I. At my grandma's house, I remember her good-tasting well water, her homemade bread, and the mounds of dishes us girls would have to wash after a huge family get-together. Two of my younger aunts teased and doted on us—always making us feel special—and they helped with the dishes. We always listened to them. We did not question them, and in some ways perhaps we obeyed them even more than our own parents. Now I know more about our traditional Dakota way of life, and how our intricate kinship system provided an abundance of mothers and fathers, sisters and brothers, aunties and uncles, and grandmas and grandpas beyond those that were directly born to us. For all intents and purposes, our aunts were and are additional mothers—even if we still call them auntie.

It was the same with our uncles. Uncle Super teased us as we ran past him, hoping to escape his infamous pinch. He laughed as he called my cousins the "Dum Dum sisters"—as in the suckers so popular at the time. I realized that all the teasing was a sign of endearment, because nestled within all the banter from our aunts and uncles were gestures of love and generosity. I have a lot of these *fun at my cousins'* memories. Still, it seems I cannot recall any stories that told me about being "Indian" or "Sioux." Storytelling and stories were what adults did when they were visiting and drinking coffee. Us kids were sent outdoors and told to *shut the door, or were you born in a barn?* So many of these memories—I realize now as I write this that they are a part of my story and connect me to my Dakota identity.

In 1975, when I was seven years old, our family moved to the farm where I spent the remainder of my childhood years. My dad's dream was to build a life much like the one he had experienced at his German-immigrant grandparents' farm. So, we left the suburban life, and Dad traded his good-paying job for raising hogs, planting crops, cutting and hauling wood, and all the never-ending work on a farm. The house my dad enthusiastically purchased must have been a hundred years old. Evidence revealed the decades it carried. For one, the place had an outhouse and a partial rock basement that would house the cords of wood needed to heat the house. The other half of the basement eventually became my mother's home hair-salon business. She acquired this skill during Indian Relocation, and it provided some pay to patch the meager farm income until she went to town for a job when I was in

My parents, Bob and Joyce Luckow, stand behind me, my brother Rob, and my banana bike. We're on our farm, posing in front of the snowball bush where we often took pictures, in about 1975.

high school. In addition to the old ladies that frequented the basement, I hold images of my aunts, cousins, and me with hair wrapped in pink, blue, and yellow rollers that held the stench of permanent solution.

As transplants to the area, I presumed we were accepted. My brother and I played with the boy and girl nearly our same age from across the highway, I babysat for a few farming families, and we went to church with some fellow Lutheran neighbors. I later came to understand that there was a lot of talk early on when we moved in, which surprised me, as nothing outward was ever displayed. But then again, this is Minnesota nice, the land of conservative Christian Scandinavians, Germans, and Poles.

While our neighbors were neighborly, some peers in school were not. I am still triggered by memories of classmates who let out war whoops and called a squaw. Teachers and the adults in my life attempted to console me, or perhaps themselves, by saying that *if I would just ignore them, it would go away.* What had taught my tormenters? Perhaps it was old John Wayne movies and TV reruns of *The Lone Ranger*, *Bonanza*, and *Gunsmoke*. One good friend—tall, skinny, blond, and blue-eyed—stood up to a girl from the "in" crowd who never seemed to tire of harassing me, the short, chubby brown girl. It seemed to me that

I was the only "Indian" in school, until my brother joined me in high school after attending a private Christian school. Yet, years later as I checked into a tribally owned hotel up north, I found myself staring at portraits of leaders on the lobby wall. I immediately recognized one picture as a brown, chubby, smiling classmate, yet now older. How did I not know he, too, was "Indian"? I wonder if he was called "chief" or tomahawk-chopped back when we were in school. Perhaps there were other Native kids in school, but I did not know it and they certainly did not align themselves. Who would? It brought on bullying and harassment. And the "Indians" or "Sioux" mentioned in class or in textbooks always seemed to be the "bad guys"—the ones starting trouble and wars. I shrank in my desk and did my best to become invisible.

As students we did not hear the truth, the whole story, about how our people were swindled from our homelands. I did not learn about how my grandpa's mother and family were forced to march to Fort Snelling in 1862. I did not hear about bounties placed on my people, or about those who fled to Canada, like my grandma's grandmother and her family. All these stories of grief and loss, resiliency and fortitude were absent from who I was as an "Indian."

My mother said she doesn't remember these family stories and wondered if they were only shared with her younger brother Super. However, some tales and fables remain with her, primarily the stories of Uŋktomi—our trickster stories. These played out through her into my upbringing. When Dad left his barn clothes on the porch and streaked through the house in his white Fruit of the Looms, she reminded us to *look the other way* or we would risk getting red eyes. Years later, I can see the connection to the Uŋktomi and the ducks story, the teaching of respecting privacy and modesty. Today, as I listen to or read the Dakota tales of our relatives, the four-legged and winged who teach us the importance of hospitality or in the raising of family, I can see now how these remnants of storytelling lived out in the dos and don'ts within and beyond my childhood.

My mother, the fifth born of nine, is the product of Indian Relocation efforts of the 1950s. Attempting to address reservation poverty through mainstream assimilation strategies, the federal government moved people from reservations to distant cities across the United States. She left Pejuhutazizi for Minneapolis, where she learned a trade: hairdressing. When she couldn't secure work upon returning to the reservation, her mother sent her to stay with her older sister in San

Francisco. There, she met my dad, who was stationed at Naval Air Station Alameda. Fate bringing two southwest Minnesotans together. They returned to Minnesota, first to Minneapolis, then the suburbs.

I once heard one of our community leaders say that no matter how long our people are gone, they come home. And so, like many others, my mother eventually returned home, as an elder, to reconnect with family, place, and memories. Given the challenges she endured, I appreciate her efforts to do what she thought best for herself and her children. She kept me connected to my relatives and this land I now call home, giving me the desire to return to a place of seasonal memories and relatives.

After high school graduation, I chose to attend the University of Minnesota Morris, about seventy miles from Pejuhutazizi. Its campus is a former Indian boarding school. In fact, it was the same Indian boarding school that some of my grandpa's siblings attended—a story I only recently uncovered. This move to the Morris campus proved to be pivotal. I was finally among other Indians. The first friend I made was from the White Earth Nation, as was my Indian counselor, who became a reliable support, helping me to navigate campus life. I did not escape racial slurs and prejudice, but I felt more power than I had before because of those around me. And once again, a tall, skinny, blond friend defended me and my heritage against people who did not even know me. The five years I spent at the university gave me foundational experiences that helped me understand that the world was multidimensional and complex. I had a chance to step away from the fishbowl experiences of my childhood school days and to find my bicultural self.

During weekends and summer breaks, I returned to my mother's relatives and land and stayed with an aunt or at my grandma's home. Finally, upon graduation, I moved there and found a job and an "Indian" to marry, just as Mom told me to do. Jason is from one of the ten or so extended families of Pejuhutazizi and the Sisseton Wahpeton Oyate (of the Lake Traverse Reservation, most often just called the Sisseton Reservation). Our life together has brought about three boys: Hunter, Tanner, and Walker.

The remainder of my professional life has been in service to Native people, as the tribe's mental health/social service worker, a postsecondary school counselor to Native students, a tribal administrator, and eventually an elected tribal leader. I've worked alongside my people—the people that claimed me, and I, them. Despite the challenges of tribal politics and family and community trauma drama, I cannot imagine being anywhere else. I can remember my grandma telling me, "Terri, we didn't think you'd come here to stay. We thought you were lost to the white world forever." This place I call home connects me to a bloodline that is sown into the land. It is where my great-great-grandmother and -grandfather returned after exile, and it is here where I have continued my bloodline.

This land is Dakota homeland, and thus the language itself is baked into the trees and waters, the four-legged and even the winged who continue to return home year after year. My curiosity about and memories of the Indian language I heard as a child remained, and I eventually pursued the yearning to speak my grandmother's first language. I remember her initial response as I expressed my desire to learn: "Oh, what do you want to learn that for? Just learn to speak good English." I was baffled at the time, but the limited stories she later shared of her boarding school experience, pieced together with research, helped me to understand just why she said that.

Still, she became my language teacher, along with my father-in-law. Learning entailed "hanging out at grandma's house," visits to relatives, listening to stories, and doing everyday activities while learning common language. With my little boys always in tow—Hunter seven, Tanner four, and Walker just a year old at that time—I found and spent time with fellow language learners and activists and those tired of mainstream systems. A group of us met at kitchen tables and eventually formed Dakota Wicoḣaŋ, Dakota Way of Life—a Native nonprofit dedicated to Dakota language and lifeways.

I was thirsty to learn what should have been my birthright: how to properly introduce myself and to know Dakota prayers, songs, commands, and common language. I learned about significant sites, place names, and plant names. I learned about our Dakota history and the common collective history from Indigenous people across the globe. I practiced, spoke, and shared my language, stumbling along with mispronunciations and words out of context. My father-in-law was ever so patient and generous with his teaching and stories. He would sit at our kitchen table for hours, drinking coffee and eating rolls while explaining a particular word or the many ways to convey a thought.

My grandma welcomed our visits, too, albeit a bit less patiently.

Caske (Hunter), Hepi (Walker), and Hepaŋna (Tanner) at the Caŋšayapi wacipi, 2002.

And so, I learned to bring a tape recorder. She taught me how to make bread, preserve plum jelly, and dry waskuya while sharing her language. She called my boys Siŋte and Taskakpa—Tail and Woodtick—as they were always right behind or attached to me. I think back on some things that now seem so amusing. Once, as Grandma became weary of pronouncing a word with gutturals for me, she said, "Gee, Terri, you're German—this should come easy for you." I am not sure if she thought the five pints of German blood that flow through me should inherently shape the guttural sounds required in both languages. While German was my great-grandmother Emma's first language, it petered out just as it did in other immigrant families who eventually accepted English only. Where Kuŋši lacked in patience, she made up in so many other ways—including how I was missing "connector words" and teaching me how to write the language, as my father-in-law could not. Later, in formal language classes with an increased focus on grammar, I found myself shaking my head at how I probably sounded like a toddler—and likely still do.

I started the language pursuit believing I would be fluent one day. Today, I have come to understand that language learning is a lifelong journey. Long after my grandma and father-in-law had passed away, another fluent elder in our community was helping Dakota Wicohaŋ with some translations for our horse program. Reluctant at first, this first-generation speaker, one of just a handful remaining in the state, told me I needed to ask an "expert." I laughed and said, "You're it!" But it was through this experience that I came to understand there isn't anyone that knows all the words to a language, and so you do the best you can—one word at a time. The precious teachings of my grandma and father-in-law fortified me as a Dakota wiŋyaŋ and ina. The language brought me so much more than the ability to speak some words. It provided me connection to the roots and stories of my relatives and a *belongingness*, no matter how the path meandered.

Some of the stories in this collection connect the dots and fill the voids and gaps of my story. Some provide insight into why things were and perhaps still are. Some stories give me a compassionate understanding of so many things. Most importantly, these stories are important to me because they tell of who I belong to. I am of the people who dig the yellow medicine and the great-great-granddaughter of Tašinasusbecawiŋ.

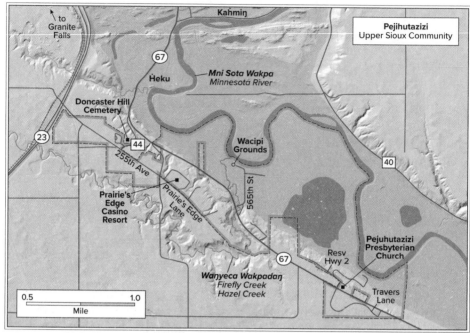

**Pejihutazizi
Upper Sioux Community**

to Granite Falls

Kahmiŋ

67

Ḣeku

Mni Sota Wakpa
Minnesota River

Doncaster Hill
Cemetery

23

44

255th Ave

Wacipi
Grounds

565th St

40

Prairie's
Edge
Casino
Resort

Prairie's Edge Lane

67

Resv
Hwy 2

Pejuhutazizi
Presbyterian
Church

Waŋyeca Wakpadaŋ
Firefly Creek
Hazel Creek

Travers
Lane

0.5   1.0
Mile

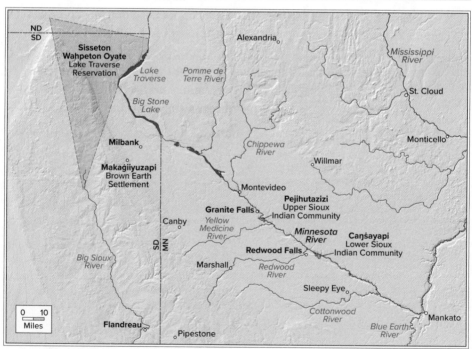

ND
SD

Alexandria

*Mississippi
River*

**Sisseton
Wahpeton Oyate**
Lake Traverse
Reservation

*Lake
Traverse*

*Pomme de
Terre River*

St. Cloud

*Big Stone
Lake*

Monticello

Milbank

*Chippewa
River*

Makaġiiyuzapi
Brown Earth
Settlement

Willmar

Montevideo

Pejihutazizi
Upper Sioux
Indian Community

SD
MN

Granite Falls

*Yellow
Medicine
River*

*Minnesota
River*

Caŋśayapi
Lower Sioux
Indian Community

Canby

*Big Sioux
River*

Redwood Falls

Marshall

*Redwood
River*

Sleepy Eye

0   10
Miles

*Cottonwood
River*

Mankato

Flandreau

Pipestone

*Blue Earth
River*

PART 2. THE VOICES

Utuhu Caŋ Cistiŋna / Teresa Peterson

You can look at a family tree and recite your genealogy. But it is not until you hear story that you become relatives.

Two main storytellers transmit the voices heard in this book: my great-grandfather Waŋbdiska, or Fred Pearsall, and my uncle Wašicuŋhdinažiŋ, Walter "Super" LaBatte Jr. These stories come from the four generations before me, from my uncle to my great-great-grandmother, all from Pejuhutazizi. Let me introduce you to them, starting in the present and moving to the past.

Wašicuŋhdinažiŋ—Walter LaBatte Jr.

Dekši Super is my mom's younger brother. He is the son of Walter and Genevieve LaBatte, born in 1948, and like most of his siblings, he came into the world at the Pipestone Indian Hospital. He graduated from Granite Falls High School and went on to earn a bachelor's degree in German from Macalester College. I consider him the brainiac of our family. He was the first in our LaBatte tiošpaye to earn a college degree. As I was getting ready to graduate high school and to be done, as in *done*, with education, Dekši—a man of few words—asked me a simple question: "Where are you going to college?" College? I hadn't even thought about going to college. No one talked to me about going to college. That one small question, his generous assumption of my abilities, took me on a trajectory of lifelong learning. He became my

The Upper Sioux Community, five miles south of Granite Falls, Minnesota, was formally established in 1938. Because of our small land base, only a small proportion of our approximately five hundred members live on tribal lands. We have a complicated legal history; many of us are enrolled as members of the Sisseton Wahpeton Oyate.

steadfast mentor. I have called on his wisdom and faithful assistance many times over. He is a straight shooter; there is no mincing of words. This character trait I have heard others describe as gruff, and in fact he has challenged my own sensitivity from time to time, to which my mom says, "He's just like Grandpa."

Dekši is an accomplished artist. I am quite sure that his beadwork, traditional brain-tanned leather, and drums are all over the planet. But he is also a generous artist, in that he willingly shares his craft, skills, and knowledge. I am grateful that one of my sons, along with other Dakota apprentices, has taken the opportunity to learn from him, so these traditions carry on.

He is our family historian. I call on Dekši for any Dakota language, culture, and history questions. He has the rare gift of memory and storytelling. I sometimes wonder who I will call when I can't call uncle anymore.

Dekši is the father of two sons, three grandchildren, and one great-grandchild. He lives with his partner, Karen Odden, in the Mni Sota River valley at Pejuhutazizi, right where he was born and raised, in a home he built with his own two hands. I stop over at his place

Dekši Super, 2010.

often, including when I need hardwood ash from his fireplace to make paṡdayapi (another tradition he is practicing and passing along). He is from the generation of Dakota people that honors the tradition of titokaŋ, visiting. That is, he welcomes unexpected callers—not like waṡicuŋ homes where you have to call ahead and make an appointment, or today's generation who just visit on social media. This reminds me so much of all the visiting to my grandma's and other elders in our community that are now gone.

Today, Dekṡi is the gifted storyteller of our family. He shares stories that he remembers and has the gift to recite, as well as reflections from generations past. He shares, "Sometimes I feel special in that my dad, my mom, my grandpa, my uncles, and other elders of my youth shared all these stories with me. Then again, maybe others were told these, too, but I am maybe the only one to remember. Anyways, I feel a responsibility to pass on those that were given to me." Wopida, Dekṡi for carrying these stories into the future.

Wihake—Genevieve Pearsall LaBatte

Dekṡi's mother, my kuŋṡi, was born in 1912 to Wakaŋtiomaniwiŋ and Waŋbdiska. She was the fifth-born daughter, thus her Dakota name, Wihake. In part, she was raised by her grandmother, Taṡinasusbe-cawiŋ, known as Susbe. Dekṡi shared this story:

> My aunt Harriet told me that after their mother—Eunice Amos Pearsall, Wakaŋtiomaniwiŋ—died, they would find my mother wandering around looking for her. Oh, how sad! My mother, the youngest of five daughters, was two years old when her mother died. Aunt Harriet said her mother was sick for a long time. After my grandmother's death, the girls were raised by their grandmother, Taṡinasusbecawiŋ, but Waŋbdiska, their dad, also raised them.

Grandma and her four older sisters, Estella, Evelyn, Harriet, and Cerisse, all attended the Pipestone Indian Boarding School. I have copies of their boarding school documents and letters between Grandpa Fred and the superintendent. Some are emotionally difficult to read. Grandma was six years old when she was enrolled at the school, and

My grandma Genevieve Pearsall LaBatte and Dekši Super, attending a LaBatte family reunion in Canada, about 1986.

she told me she was so young she had to stay with the matrons. Over the years, she described her experience as mostly positive, because she appreciated learning to cook and sew. She also shared with me that she was perhaps treated more fairly because her father was white. Later, she and her sister entered eighth grade at Granite Falls High School and were the first Native graduates. I worked in Indian education at the very same school, supporting Native students to see that they graduated. I felt connected and purposeful when I saw the plaque that recorded their names first in the list of Native graduates.

My grandma Genevieve Pearsall and grandpa Walter LaBatte married in Sisseton, South Dakota, in December 1934. They had nine children: Wayne, Gary (who died as an infant), Juanita, Gordy, my mom Joyce, Walter Jr. (Super), Julie, Sarah, and Debra. Genevieve's father, Grandpa Fred, gave them all Dakota names. How they raised all those children in a two-bedroom house seems unimaginable. Later, they also raised three grandchildren.

After I had my own kids, I wanted to learn the Dakota language in part so they would always know who they are. My grandma, despite her time at boarding school, retained her Dakota language. Yet my mom said that when she was growing up, her mother and father primarily spoke Dakota when they didn't want the kids to know what they were saying. Before my grandma's passing in 2010, she and just a handful of first-generation Dakota speakers remained in Minnesota. She generously shared her language, stories, and humor as an advisor to Dakota Wicohaŋ. In 2008, when we at Dakota Wicohaŋ interviewed her and many of the remaining Dakota elders, all first-generation speakers of the language, she shared, "This language here, I think it's spiritual." I hold precious memories of her final days in the hospital as she sang to me from her *Dakota Odowaŋ*. Undoubtedly, she helped play a role in the Dakota language revitalization movement going on today.

Grandma has been gone for over ten years now, but I continue to draw on so many memories and enjoy reminiscing with those that remember her—especially how funny she was. Recently, Ma was talking about the white gloves Grandma liked wearing, and next we were laughing about how she regressed to brown chore gloves late in life. That was the day when Ma gave me Grandma's journal—if you can call it that. Not like some of the handsome journals often gifted, but a small notebook, with the Dueber's Department Store eighty-nine-cent sticker pasted on the front and her pen still in the spiral ring. Her recognizable cursive writing, challenging to read, included shorthand notes. She jotted down the comings and goings of people, trips to town and amounts spent on purchases, random blood sugar recordings, and amounts she borrowed to children and grandchildren. Her writing rarely shared her opinion on things, and there was no gossip or juicy story, other than an occasional note about a relative who ended up in jail. It contained just the routine of her life. Though maybe the mundane should, too, be acknowledged and perhaps celebrated because it also tells a story. Sometimes there is a story not necessarily told by the writer, but one formed by the reader. The journal revealed to me what my grandma valued—visits, conversations, and time spent with people. It affirmed for me of what Icepaŋsi Gaby Strong has shared with me, that we are supposed to be medicine for each other. Wopida, Grandma, for all your good medicine.

Tiwakaŋhokšina—Walter LaBatte Sr.

My grandpa was born in 1900, the youngest child to Sarah Renville and Philip LaBatte. Sarah was the daughter of Tiwakaŋ, aka Gabriel Renville, and Tuŋkaŋmaniwiŋ; her Dakota name, Sagadašiŋ, comes from the Ojibwe word for British. Philip raised and sold race horses. Dekši's genealogy has traced another three generations back to Tataŋka Mani, or Walking Buffalo. And Philip's parents were Mary Ironshield and Francois LaBatte (son of Angelique and Michel LaBatte). I share these names as you will read about some of these people in the stories.

My grandpa is remembered as a gifted storyteller and promoter of traditional ways. I have heard many stories of Grandpa from family members and others, but my own memories of him are far fewer than those I have of Grandma. He had a giant white horse, Thunder, who everyone seems to remember. He found an excuse every day to go to town. He was a hard worker and a great conversationalist. Grandpa

Walter LaBatte Sr. with his horse Thunder.

displayed a level of contentment that has stuck with me. Grandpa was like that saying—people might forget what you said or what you did, but they never forget how you made them feel. When you came to visit Grandpa, he lit up and was genuinely happy to see you. He greeted you with a kind of "Oh-oh-oh hah," and a little laughter, emitting a sense that he had been waiting for you. He provided prayer and common sense (like "Too much of anything isn't good") and was the glue for our LaBatte tioŝpaye. The South Dakota Oral History Center has some interviews with him, recorded in 1968. It was magical to listen again to his unique voice. He shared stories about his life and stories his mother told him as a boy. He spoke of his experiences and of times we only read about in textbooks: his brother dying from the flu during the 1918 pandemic, getting married during the Depression, surviving the drought of the 1930s, and not being able to find work. My favorite is when he is talking about his children and how one of his daughters just had a little girl.

Wakaŋtiomaniwiŋ—Eunice Amos

My great-grandmother Wakaŋtiomaniwiŋ was born in 1882, the daughter to Taŝinasusbecawiŋ and Hotoŋtoŋna. Her beautiful Dakota name translates as Spirit Walking in the House, and her English name was Eunice Amos. A family Bible records her marriage to Grandpa Fred: "April 28, 1900 heehaŋ Eunice W. Amos qa Fredric W. Pearsall kiciyuzapi." They traveled and lived in various places, including Sisseton, South Dakota, and Santee, Nebraska, due to his role as a translator. They had five daughters: Estella, Evelyn, Harriet, Cerisse, and my grandma Genevieve. But Wakaŋtiomaniwiŋ died of food poisoning on September 22, 1914, shortly after my grandma was born. Each time I look at her picture, I can see features that are carried on through family members, like her cheeks and other facial features. And of course, my cousin carries her beautiful name. But most of all, despite her unfortunate early death, I can see the inheritance she provided: the oodles of cousins and relatives yet to come.

Eunice Amos and Fred Pearsall in their wedding photo, 1900.

Waŋbdiska—Fred Pearsall

My great-grandfather Waŋbdiska was a white man. But for reasons be-yond blood quantum, he lived his life as a Dakota. He spoke Dakota, lived with the Dakota, and was an ally to the Dakota. Grandpa Fred, as my mom, uncle, and aunts call him, was born in 1877 at Lac qui Parle to Francis and Estella Pearsall. His father, Francis Pearsall, was from a wealthy family in Bainbridge, New York; in 1873 Francis married Es-tella Parsons, and the couple moved to Minnesota and lived in an old hotel in Lac qui Parle. Shortly after Fred's birth, they moved to Granite Falls, where they built a large house west of the Great Northern Depot. Fred's father was the cashier of the Yellow Medicine Bank from 1884 to 1886, when the family moved to Minneapolis.

On one of my visits with Cerisse, she gave me an old hand-blown glass bottle with layers of varied hues of sand from Miniȟaȟa— Minnehaha Falls—that her dad had made as a boy. Fred also learned and spoke different languages, including Latin, French, and Dakota, and he attended the University of Minnesota. After he and Eunice mar-ried in 1900, they lived in Santee, then Sisseton; after her death, he

Waŋbdiska, my great-grandfather Fred Pearsall, about 1920.

and his five daughters moved back to Granite Falls. He married Jennie Enoch, also a Dakota woman, but she, too, soon died. He was a mail carrier, and he did some work for the government as a translator. In 1941, he married Jane Brown, an Anishinaabe woman who mom and her siblings simply call Grandma Jane. In his later years, he raised vegetables in a big garden and sold them in town.

Fred lived among the Dakota people for fifty years. He took great interest in the historical events among our people. His fluency and literacy in the Dakota language was valuable to many, including the late Danny Seaboy, a Dakota elder from Sisseton who told me of his visits to see the "old man," who would "take out a hand drum from under his bed to sing and share story and language." He is remembered as a strong advocate for the Dakota people, traditions, and language, and he was often heard reprimanding the younger generation in the community: "Dakota ia. Wašicuŋ iešni!" "Speak Dakota. Don't speak English!" His beautifully handwritten notes of Dakota place names are housed in the Gale Family Library of the Minnesota History Center (and we include them here, in "Stories Tell of Place"). I understand that the late Paul Durand, who compiled a book of Native place names in Minnesota called *Where the Waters Gather and the Rivers Meet*, learned some of the names from these notes. Grandpa's role as a community historian is also shown through his response in 1918 to the Pipestone Indian Agency superintendent: "enclosed herewith a census of the Granite Falls band of Sioux Indians as per your request," he wrote, and he details the names and ages of everyone living here at the time. I was impressed when reading about his memorial service of 1959, a year after his death. There were visitors from Prairie Island and Sisseton, and the whole day was dedicated to him, with two church services, meals, and gifts bestowed in his honor.

Some stories of Grandpa Fred's come from stories he heard as a young man among the Dakota people and from his mother-in-law, Tašinasusbecawiŋ. On February 24, 1955, a few years before he died, he wrote a letter to his daughters detailing their mother's family history and sharing the many Dakota stories he heard over the years, noting, "Something over 40 years ago, I made short-hand notes of several historical tales which I heard among the old Dakota people." His stories provide insight into early Dakota life and encounters with other tribes, white people, and life's challenges. Fred shared, "Your grandmother lived a long and a very eventful life about which you girls know almost nothing, but I have heard her tell of so many events of her life that I wish to pass them on to you girls."

Tašinasusbecawiŋ—Her Dragonfly Shawl Woman

My great-great-grandmother Tašinasusbecawiŋ was born a twin near Pine Island into Wapahaša's village around 1850. While we cannot be certain of her mother's and father's names, we understand her maternal grandparents were Wiŋpteca (Short Woman) and Wayahuġa (Cruncher); her father may be Tacaŋhpikokipapi, They Are Afraid of His War Club. (Grandpa Fred's wording is ambiguous.) Her name loosely translates as Her Dragonfly Shawl (or Blanket) Woman; however, she was commonly referred to as Susbe. (*Susbeca* means "dragonfly.") As with many during that time, she did not have a birth certificate. While her gravestone shows 1845 as her date of birth and her death certificate shows 1851, a 1900 census gives it as 1850, and family story affirms this last date, as during the US–Dakota War of 1862 she was ten or twelve years of age.

Susbe married three times. She married Maĥpiya Waśtedaŋ, who took the English name of James Donnelly, on October 8, 1871. The *Iapi Oaye,* the Dakota-language newspaper published by missionaries, records them having a child, who we understand to be named Guy Donnelly, on August 19, 1877, in Flandreau, who lived for about thirty years. Maĥpiya Waśtedaŋ died suddenly while visiting relatives and is buried over by Buffalo Lake on the Sisseton Reservation. Susbe then married Hotoŋtoŋna in 1884. Hotoŋtoŋna took the English name of Joseph Amos; thus, she took the name of Alice Amos. We know through census records that she had eight children in all, including Hannah, who died in 1884; Hezekiah, a little boy who died at one year old in 1890; and Agnes, who was baptized in 1891. Yet only Eunice, Wakaŋtiomaniwiŋ, survived. Hotoŋtoŋna died in 1899. In 1904, Susbe married a Presbyterian minister named Mazaowaŋca (Iron All Over), whose English name was Rev. William O. Rogers, and she thus became Alice Rogers. She died October 26, 1927, and she, Hotoŋtoŋna, and Mazaowaŋca are all buried at Pejuhutazizi in the cemetery on the hill.

Most of what I know of my great-great-grandmother comes through written documents, like the *Iapi Oaye,* census and probate records, and a couple of rare pictures. I have a grainy copy of a photograph of her: she has a fatigued look on her face as she sits, propping her elbow on her knee, with the palm of her hand under her chin and the side of her face. I imagine that tired look is a result of all the events and experiences of war, refuge, starting over, longing, loss, grief—as well as acceptance, contentment, relief, and perhaps bittersweet joy as she looked on to her daughter and five granddaughters. There would be more tragedy in her long life after the day of that photograph. Shortly after, her daughter died, leaving those five little girls motherless. I display this picture next to an old two-quart cast-iron pot that Ma gave me, telling me that her

Tašinasusbecawiŋ, Her Dragonfly Shawl Woman, with her daughter Eunice, right, and granddaughters Estella and Evelyn, in back, and Harriet, Genevieve, and Cerisse. Eunice died shortly after this photo was taken.

mother used to play with it as a child. This pot was Susbe's. I pick up that pot from time to time, lifting it by the wire handle and running my fingers over the big crack in the bottom. I imagine the weathered hands of my great-great-grandmother and the tiny palms and fingers of my grandma. I hope to pass this pot on to a future granddaughter, though it is Susbe's stories, shared with Grandpa Fred, that I treasure the most, that will live beyond her lifetime.

PART 3. THE STORIES

....

Waŋbdiska / Fred Pearsall and Waśicuŋhdinażiŋ / Walter "Super" LaBatte Jr.

*Remember in school, when you were taught how to write a story or orga-
nize a presentation? First explain to your audience what the story is about,
next share the story, and then be sure to conclude by telling the audience
what the story was about. This approach to writing or presenting is very
explicit, requires limited critical thinking, and leaves little to the imagination—little room for readers or listeners to garner their own meaning.*

*The collection you are about to read does not use a predictable Western
approach to storytelling. Drop any expectations you may have. Sometimes one storyteller will talk for a long time, sometimes the other will.
Some stories will be repeated, told in different places by both storytellers. It
will help you to remember the people who are introduced in Part 2, but
you do not need to know all the answers right now. Be open to what the
stories may reveal for you.*

*You only need to remember that Waŋbdiska, Grandpa Fred, is writing
to his daughters. Grandpa Fred speaks first, and his words have a light
gray background. Waśicuŋhdinażiŋ, Dekśi Super, speaks next, and his
words are not shaded. He sometimes throws in a surprising word, just to
see if you're paying attention.*

*Come, let us gather around the fire for some storytelling—stories wo-
ven across time and people. Quiet your mind. Listen with your heart.
Shh. It's time now. Let's listen to Grandpa Fred and Dekśi tell stories.
We'll see you on the other side of the moon.*

Stories Impart Values

*Stories impart the values of a community, reminding us how to live and
be with each other. The Dakota, and perhaps other Native communities,
espouse seven core values: wooŋsida (compassion), woohoda (respect),
woksape (wisdom), woohitika (courage or bravery), wowaciŋtaŋka (patience), ohaŋwaśte (generosity), and waihakta (humility). Yet there are
many others that guide how we live in the world and with each other.*

Woohitika—Courage, Bravery

During the summer of 1862, your grandmother's father with some others went to the pipestone quarry to dig stone, which they were expecting to make pipes of. They had several ponies with them, and they started for home at Pejuhutazizi. They came across the hills and arrived at about where the town of Russell stands. There from the top of the hills is a magnificent view of the flat country toward the east, where the Redwood Agency stood.

There, in what appeared to be about the location of the agency, a great column of smoke was rising toward the sky. They wondered what could have happened. What was it that was burning that could make such a smoke?

Of course, they traveled slowly, as their ponies were loaded with pipestone. After a couple of days, they arrived at home and found that the traders and crooked officials had got a kind of a war started against the tribe, as they wanted to get possession of the land that was contained in their reservation along the river land—if possible, they wished to exterminate the whole tribe. This smoke which they had seen was from the burning of the traders' stores and agency buildings, which the Indians had set on fire in the course of the war which was started.

• • • •

We believe that Susbe's father was Tacaŋhpi Kokipapi, but Grandpa Fred's writings are not explicit. The Pipestone quarry, now Pipestone National Monument, is about seventy miles southwest of Upper Sioux Agency. The town of Russell is about fifty miles from Lower Sioux.

On the morning of August 18, 1862, after terrible provocation, Dakota warriors attacked Lower Sioux Agency, also known as Redwood Agency, killing many traders and government employees and burning the buildings. Most whites considered this to be the start of the US–Dakota War; some Dakota people say that the war started much earlier.

[Dekṡi Super speaks here.] Susbe and her dad had reached the coteau that overlooked the prairie. They could see smoke in the east, toward their home at Wapahaṡa's Village at the Lower Sioux Agency. They encountered a Dakota on horseback and asked him about the smoke. He told them not to go back there, that a war has started. There they buried their pipestone and fled toward the northwest.

• • • •

The only thing to do now was to move away from their homes and go toward the west and get away from the white man's army which was coming now. So, the pipestone which they had brought home was buried near one of the earthen lodges of the village.

Then all the inhabitants of the village left and went toward the west. Their first stop seems to have been up on the hill here near the cemetery and the old Riggs mission. There were several buildings at that mission, one a small building used as a schoolhouse. One afternoon, some children were playing with fire near this schoolhouse.

Someone said the children should not do that, as they might set the building on fire. Then the mother of one of the children got angry and said that her child could do as he pleased, as she was not going to scold him on account of some white man's property. Thereupon she went up to the children and took their fire and scattered it up along the building and set it on fire so that it burned down. Your grandmother seems to have been alone with her father.

They seemed to have camped for a few days in this location by the Riggs mission, and then they moved again and camped near Montevideo. They stayed there several days, and then the army caught up with them. In this location, practically the whole tribe was camped, besides the band that your grandmother belonged to. The others were

The Hazelwood Republic, established in 1854 by farming Dakota families who were led by Presbyterian missionary Stephen R. Riggs, was about six miles northwest of Yellow Medicine Agency at Hazel Creek, now the site of the Upper Sioux Community.

The camp near Montevideo, known by the whites as Camp Release, contained a large number of Dakota who were not involved in the fighting. Susbe's family probably escaped from the camp or fled west before the surrender, as General Henry Sibley's forces did not permit people to leave. The military separated 392 men from their families, imprisoned them, and began trying them, sentencing 303 to death by hanging; 38 were hanged at Mankato on December 26, 1862, which remains the largest mass hanging in US history. In November Sibley's forces marched more than 1,600 women, children, and elders to Fort Snelling, where they were held in a concentration camp beneath the bluff until the next spring, then shipped to the Crow Creek Reservation. The men who had not been hanged were imprisoned at Camp Kearney, still under death sentences, until 1866, when President Andrew Johnson ordered remission of their sentences. In the summer of 1863, Sibley and other US forces pursued the Dakota who fled into Dakota Territory. In these "punitive expeditions," the US military attacked camps of Lakota, Yanktonnai, and Yankton people, as well.

holding a great many prisoners which they had taken in the raids, mostly women and children.

Your grandmother and family with their old neighbors left and wandered around, hunting and fishing and trapping. The next spring, they started toward the west. They arrived somewhere up in the Red River Valley and were camped one night on a slight rise of ground with no trees, but there was a shallow ravine to one side, and beyond the ravine was a strip of timber.

One morning, a company of soldiers all of a sudden came into sight to fight them. This was a surprise attack.

Everyone immediately left the camp and ran across the ravine and took shelter in the timber: men, women, children, and all. The men took their guns with them, as they knew the soldiers had come for a fight. When they got over to the woods, they found that the men had forgotten a sack of bullets for their guns. They did not know what to do. Finally, your grandmother volunteered to run back across the ravine and get the sack of bullets. She was very swift of foot when she was young—but as you girls remember her, she would not have been very swift, as when she got old, she was very fleshy.

She ran across the ravine and up to the tents and grabbed the bag of bullets, and as she was running back to the timber, the soldiers began shooting at her and several bullets came very close to her. This shows how brave white-man soldiers were to shoot at a young girl in that way. There was a little skirmish with the soldiers, but there was no report of any damage, and the soldiers did not pursue them anymore. Many years afterward, one of the men of that party was talking about the episode, but he did not know for sure who the girl was that retrieved the bag of bullets. Grandma spoke up and said that she was the one, and they all knew what a dangerous mission she accomplished with the brave soldiers shooting at her.

• • • •

My maternal great-grandmother, Tašinasusbecawiŋ, was twelve years old when this happened, according to Grandpa. She and her family were fleeing Minnesota and were camping in the Red River Valley when they were attacked by the army. The menfolk in her family were running out of ammunition, as the extra was still tied on their horses' bags. My twelve-year-old great-grandmother volunteered to retrieve the ammo while the army was shooting at her. She'd learned to run in a zigzag fashion to escape the bullets, a well-known tactic of the Dakota, as my grandfather said. She was successful in retrieving the ammo, and they were successful in blunting the attack. Years later, when Great-Grandmother was old, she heard a retelling of this attack by a participant, a onetime army man. She got up and said she was the twelve-year-old that he was shooting at.

Wookiya—Helping Others, Being Helpful

When I moved home in 2001, our fields were much like every other field in that lots of chemical fertilizer and pesticides and weed killer had been used on them. After I quit renting out my fields, I put them in restored prairie, and I amended the soil for my garden by adding

a lot of organic material—sphagnum peat moss and horse manure—
so my soil is now soft and fertile, and the weeds pull up easily.

This sparked a memory from my preteen or early teenage years.
Bob St. Claire and his family moved into town, so they did not have
garden space. So, some wašicuŋ farmer let them use his barnyard for
the garden. It was full of rotten manure, and the ground was much
like mine now. Bob and his family went out to the garden, and I
helped them weed. Man, it was easy to weed—much different than
ours at home. I came back home all enthusiastic to tell my parents
about it. Our wašicuŋ minister was there, and he killed all my joy
by saying, "Why don't you do that at home?" I guess he was right; I
probably was lazy at home. I think my parents were rather astounded
at his scolding, but they said nothing. I guess this was our Dakota
values (helping) coming into conflict with wašicuŋ values. My intent
was to tell my folks how good the soil was, and maybe we could also
have such soil.

· · · ·

Many years ago, I was at a funeral led by an Episcopal minister, and
the family asked for the Presbyterian Hymn #114, "Beautiful River,"
to be sung. The minister, of course, was not familiar with the Dakota
Presbyterian hymns, and there was no piano or music, so he asked
if anyone knew that hymn and could help lead the song. Of course,
being raised with these songs, I knew the tune and song but waited
for someone older than me to speak up, since I always respected the
age protocol. I was too shy, I suspect, so did not volunteer, and no one
else did, either. To this day, I always regretted not helping this family.
A similar incident happened with our Dakota Odowaŋ #27, and again
I did not speak up. The piano player said that the music did not fit the
words to the song, but they did because you sang the verses over and
over. But again, he was not familiar with Presbyterian Dakota hymns.
So, my advice to the young: if you can help, do it, and don't be intimi-
dated by the elder protocol.

Miniheca—Working Hard, Being Active

I used to hear my mother and aunt talk about someone saying, "He,
John, nina miniheca." That means that John is not lazy, he's a hard

worker, always doing something, being active. I always wanted to be that—what my mother and aunt considered a good attribute.

In relative terms, compared to today's youth, it would appear that I had a hard life—cutting wood, farming, walking home after sports. But I appreciate the work ethic I was taught, the sense of responsibility instilled in me, so I would not exchange that experience for anything. Besides, I heard what my older brothers went through when farming with horses, and in comparison, my life was a walk in the park. My brother Wayne—or Mato, as he was often called by his Dakota name—told a story of my mom also working in the fields on the farm, besides her inside duties. This event occurred when they were haying with the team of horses, Tom and Jerry, as they were called. She was raking, and as she was driving the team, a pheasant flew up and scared the horses. My mom had a runaway team and she fell off the back. That was before my time, so I have a hard time imagining Mom doing that kind of work. I suppose, though, at the end of the day her work did not end—she had cooking and housework to do. A whole different era.

• • • •

When I was about twelve years old, I was the man of the house, responsible for keeping the house warm while Dad was on a high-line job far away, as he was out two weeks at a time. We had a wood furnace in the basement where we stored all our wood. By the second Friday, we were almost out of wood, so I told Dad about it that Friday night. He said he had wood cut in the pasture and we would get it on Saturday. Because it was winter, the tractor did not start, so we had to use a sled to haul it in. Oh man, it was cold out, so one round I stayed in to warm up, and my mom saw out the kitchen window that he was pulling it all by himself, and where was I? She scolded me for not helping, so I went out and told him I was cold; he said nothing, no scolding. He had a job to do, and that was the way Dad was.

Dad was a lineman, a member of International Brotherhood of Electrical Workers Local 160 out of Minneapolis. He told me the union came out to the reservations after World War II recruiting Indians to help build the electric grid. Their assumption was that they were following in the steps of the Mohawk Indians who built the skyscrapers of New York—the assumption being that Indians were not scared of heights. Dad said that he was just as scared as the white man, but he could not pass up the big money, so that was his trade, along with farming. My oldest brother also went into that trade. One time, I went with Dad to the union hall to sign up for work, and the union official looked at me and said, "Is this our next lineman?" I said, "No, I am going to college. I'm not working outside in the winter." Dad had told me how hard it was working outside in the winter, with no shelter, eating their lunch outside. So I went to college, got my BA from Macalester, and ended up working construction just like my dad.

Some twenty or thirty years ago, a man that worked with my dad on the highlines said to me (I am sure he was referring to my education), "You can't hold a candle to your dad." The others around me started to defend me, but I did not take his statement as anything other than a compliment to my dad. I have told others of this story, and they have taken it as a slam to me. I have never been in competition with my dad but have a complete admiration of him for raising all of us kids plus three grandchildren—with his eighth-grade or maybe even sixth-grade education.

Walter LaBatte Sr. and Walter LaBatte Jr., about 1965.

There are a few Dakota men who remind me of my dad for being physically active into their eighties, like my dad who was still cutting wood to heat the house. Men like Vine Marks, Joe Williams, and of course Emmett Eastman. I look up to them and hope I, too, can still be around and active. See, we Dakota men don't all have to die in our forties but can live long if we take care of what we put into our bodies and keep physically active. I suspect it is part genetics, but I think our lifestyles have more to do with it. So, we need to get away from the "Live hard, die young, and leave a beautiful memory" sentiment.

• • • •

Dad told me this story. About 1905, his mother, Sarah Renville La-Batte, took her two sons, Sidney and Walter, to visit their paternal grandmother, Mary Ironshield LaBatte, at Lower Sioux. They took the Milwaukee railroad from Sisseton (maybe from Peever, South Dakota) to Olivia, Minnesota. She then hired a sleigh and team to take them to Lower Sioux, about sixteen miles. This was obviously in the winter. This seems quite an undertaking compared to my concerns of hiring a taxi to get from airport to hotel or from train station to hotel. That about puts everything in perspective: if Grandma can do this in 1905, I surely should be able to do this today. Especially taking into consideration she spoke only Dakota.

• • • •

One time when I was growing up, I saw Dad sewing. I don't remember what, maybe his dance outfit or mending his clothes. At the time, I wondered why Mom wasn't doing that, as that seemed to be her job. Later on, I discovered that Dad learned to be a tailor at Flandreau Indian School. That seemed to be so incongruous with Dad as a farmer, highline worker, and construction worker. He said they went to school half a day and then worked on the school's farm. I guess they raised cattle and the feed for such.

Flandreau Indian School, established in 1871 as a Presbyterian mission church, was purchased by the federal government in 1883 and became a boarding school in 1892. By 1929, it was teaching students through grade twelve.

I often wonder if my two sons will marvel at the things I know how to do—maybe not, since I have been openly sharing. But I marvel at Dad's talents, as he never openly shared with us until prompted. One of them was the making of buckskin. He never shared until I asked him. How could he know this and not tell us? Another time, my cousin Robin Blue and I were playing around with a lasso—playing cowboy, I guess, in our yard. Dad happened by and saw what we were doing. He said, "Let me see that"—he meant the lasso. He grabbed it and started twirling it into a circle and jumped in and out of the twirling circle and did other tricks with it. Just as I had seen Will Rogers do in films. Will had nothing on Dad. Robin and I were astounded at Dad's tricks. Dad gave back the lasso and said nothing as he walked away. What hidden talents does your dad know or have? Better find out while he is still here.

• • • •

Dekši Super and Robin Blue,
about 1964.

Twenty-some years ago, I saw my son looking enviously at those champion dancers who won the competitions at powwows every weekend. He was a good dancer, too, and would place, but I knew he wanted to move up to be one of those champions. I could see he wanted the glory and money. I told him that everything that glittered was not gold and that some of those champions had to borrow money the next weekend to get to the powwow. I told him it was a much more reliable and stable life to get a job and work—to develop a good work ethic, as Dad told me. To my surprise, my son followed my advice by working every day to provide for his family. I am so proud of him for still dancing, but not to be a pro. Couple years ago, I asked if he was going to the Prairie Island powwow. He said, "No, I would like to, but I have to work." That made me proud that he took his job seriously. And the stability shows in that his girls all are doing well in school.

Ohaŋwaśte—Generosity

Another Dakota word from yesteryear appeared in my consciousness: ohaŋśica, which means stingy, illiberal (not liberal). When I was young, I never wanted to hear that charge about me, to be stingy and not generous. All it took was to hear the last part of the word, śica, which means bad. So, here's the local to the national in reference to this word. Some years ago, the tribe sent out a notice of some coming event or benefit. It stated, "For Upper Sioux members and spouses only." My mother's reaction was "Now that's ohaŋśica. Even before the casino, when we had little, we would never put that restriction on. We are Dakota, we are generous, ohaŋwaśte is us." Now, ohaŋśica thinking is also in "Putting America first and to H. with others' suffering." That is also about homeless vets not getting shelter because there are so-called immigrants. Why do we want to lessen our care for humanity? One is more important than the other? I also figured out my mother is bringing these words to me.

Woohoda—Respect

Having grown up in this small community of Pejuhutazizi, I know the "pecking order" of the elders, merely because I know who was ahead of me in school, so I give deference to those older than me. I recognized that concept even as a youngster, as I would see my parents do that to those older than them. And I gave deference to these elders without disrespecting my parents. Nature took its course by finally placing my parents as the eldest in our tribe, and I saw that respect given them (my dad lived to ninety-five and my mom to ninety-seven). Those were the unwritten rules of our community. I wonder if that still exists today, or is it merely paid lip service? And if so, I can accept that, as there have been so many changes in our society today.

• • • •

There was a family here in my youth who used to call their parents "the old man" and "the old lady." Oh, my mom would get upset about that and scolded us kids never to show the disrespect by calling Mom or Dad that, so we never used those terms. I wonder if anyone still uses those terms in referring to your parents or spouse. Now using the Dakota term Wakaŋkadaŋ or Uŋkaŋna is fine, considering they both may mean that, but they are terms of endearment.

Wowaditake—Fortitude

With these times of extremely cold weather, I wonder about our ancestors and how they coped. My dad, born 1900, told me when he was young, his parents sent him to live with some relatives who lived in a tipi. He said they banked snow up against the tipi and that it was actually quite warm and comfortable that winter.

Waihakta—Humility

There is a well-told story in Alcoholics Anonymous (AA) of a person responding to the issue of humility, of being humble, when he said, "Humility is my strong suit." That and the self-proclamation of being an Ikce Wicaṡta, a Common Man, are meant to be lived and not self-proclaimed. In other words, the self-statement nullifies the fact, to my way of thinking.

• • • •

April 4, 1986, was a Friday, and the two previous days I drank. On this day I chanced it again to drink and went to the Woodshed Bar in St. Paul. By this time, I really had to monitor my drinking because if I drank too much, I would end up back in the hospital with pancreatitis. So, the next day, I knew that I was headed to the hospital because I could feel the early stages of an attack. That day, I was so sick that there was no thought of drinking. I was lower than whale shit, as the saying goes, and I cried out to Wakaŋtaŋka to help me quit. I made a bargain with her that if she healed me from not having an attack, I really would quit. So, the following days were an almost constant state of prayers for me. I ended up not getting an attack, and I continued with my sobriety without going to treatment. But early on in my recovery, I often heard the question "Do you remember your last drunk? And if you don't remember, you haven't had it." Wow, that hit me like a ton of bricks. I became determined never to forget this episode, as I never want to go back to that *hell*. So, the question is "Can you remember your last drunk?" I shall never forget that first month of struggle; it saved my life.

Wapidapi—Gratitude

When I was in high school or thereabouts, Dad was off working the highlines when I needed new shoes, as the sole was coming off mine. I pleaded with Mom for a new pair of shoes, and she finally relented, using her last twenty-dollar bill. Dang, I don't remember being very grateful for that. I wish for some way that I could go back to them days and shower my folks with C-notes to ease their life. I am not very proud of taking Mom's last twenty-dollar bill. I am so grateful, though, for all their teachings and encouragement to get an education, thus making life easier for me.

• • • •

Shortly after I sobered up, I told my mom not to jinx me by complimenting me, as I took that as a sure challenge to my sobriety. So, my mom never told me she was proud of me for sobering up. However, she told my wife at the time that she was very happy and proud for me. So, when I came home to visit from the Cities, I always gave my mother money. I came home one time and was giving her money and she said no, that they were fine. I never realized that our little casino was very successful. So, I am glad that near the end of their lives, my parents did not have financial worries.

I feel fortunate that I have and enjoy material things which my parents never had. I have a heated garage so I don't have to deal with the car not starting in the cold weather, I have a wood splitter—no splitting wood by hand—and I have a reliable tractor with a snowplow. I have a college education. All these things make life easier for me. Looking to the future, will my two sons have it easier than me? I hope so. What do you think about your children? Will they have it better?

• • • •

On my walks, I start out with a prayer of gratitude, which opens my mind to empty it of any remaining negativity, leaving space for intuition, inspiration, and creativity. This is where I meet Wakaŋtaŋka. This is what I call my meditative walk. In no time, it seems, I have my six-mile walk in. I take care of my physical health as well as the spiritual.

Is it possible to hold seemingly diametrically opposite views simultaneously? Such as having a view or wish for a long life and the same time wishing for rest from a weary life? I remember my ninety-some-year-old dad saying, "Thank you, Wakaŋtaŋka, for seeing me through the night that I can enjoy and experience another day of your creation, but I am ready anytime, Wakaŋtaŋka." I understand that and use the same words often. Will it ever come a time when you think, "Man, I have been at this party too long; I need to move on"? And then not be shamed for such? I learned so much about life from my parents.

Mitakuye Owasiŋ—All My Relations

I asked my aunt one time why she called her granddaughter Uŋcidaŋ, which means little grandmother—*uŋci* is grandmother, *daŋ* is a diminutive ending. My aunt explained it this way. My cousins lost their mother and came to live with my aunt—their grandmother. During this time, my cousin, who was five or six years old and the eldest of the three, took great care of her younger siblings and acted, as my aunt said, like a caring lil' grandmother. So today in church, I was reminded of this, as Uŋcidaŋ has taken up the role of her grandmother, my aunt, by being a great leader and supporter of our Pejuhutazizi Presbyterian Church. Thanks, Uŋcidaŋ.

• • • •

One year at Rapid City, I stopped at a gas station to put air in my truck's tires. The new trucks now tell you when and which tire is low, so I was doing that maintenance when an old wašicuŋ guy came in to do the same. I could tell there was no way he could do the job of getting down—and more importantly, getting back up—so I told him I would put air in his tires. He thanked me and drove off. I was remembering all the stories I had heard of racists in Rapid City and wondered if he were one. But it made no difference to me, as he was someone, an elder, in need. And I really kind of thought I wished he were one, as my gesture might have changed his mind. At least I would have no shame or guilt in my heart. Mitakuye owasiŋ—we are all related, all children of God deserving of respect, even though it may not be returned.

• • • •

Here is an interesting comparison. Recently, I watched an interview with Neil deGrasse Tyson about his book *Astrophysics for People in a Hurry.* He says that all of the universe is made up of the same four elements: carbon, oxygen, hydrogen, and nitrogen. That is the basis for the saying that we are made up of stardust. That reminded me of our Dakota saying and philosophy of mitakuye owasiŋ—we are all related. We are related to all the human family, to the buffalo, birds, and all of the animal family, but also to all the rocks, trees, and everything else. In other words, all of creation, we are the same. Science caught up to Dakota spirituality.

Stories Transmit Traditions

Stories pass on ways of being and doing things. They can be as simple as teaching the origin of a tradition, bringing clarity and purpose to one's practice. They can also be complex and labor intensive, delivering time-honored, beautiful results. Dekši Super's writing, in particular, addresses the traditional practices that he has learned and carries on. Some of his stories teach about our language. Stories of traditions also

shape identities and remind us of what makes people into family and
community. Dakota traditions, while they are ever changing, continue to
be passed down through each generation and are shared through story.
We have many traditions—thus, many stories are shared here.

The Buffalo Hunt

This story was told by Tasinasusbecawiŋ, my mother-in-law by my first
wife, in about the year 1912 or 1913. The events told had occurred in the
early 1850s. This is a story concerning the Titoŋwaŋ people out west
along the Missouri River and is about a calamity which they encountered with the elements. In fact, the eastern Dakota people often spoke
of some of the terrible encounters which the western people had with
nature and in which a great many lives were sometimes lost. It seems
as if the elements are particularly ferocious and unpredictable on the
open western prairies.

Long ago, it was a custom among the Dakota and probably among
other tribes for a person or a group of people to go visiting to a neighboring tribe or band and stay a year or two and then return home. In
such cases, relationships were established; for instance, a man would
take some man as his brother or cousin or "friend," or a woman taking
some woman as her sister or cousin.

Such relationships were remembered to the second or third generation, and afterward many happy meetings took place as a result of
such relationships being established. Even to the present day, such relationships sometimes pose a quandary to the US Indian agencies in
establishing proper heirship to the estates of dead Indian allottees.

One summer at the time of this tale, a Santee or Mdewakaŋtoŋwaŋ
party of six persons whose home was in the vicinity of Mankato, Min-
nesota, made such a trip. They started from their home in southern
Minnesota and traveled straight west across the country, passing near
Flandreau, South Dakota, and on to the west until they came to the
Missouri River, where they contacted a village of the western people.

This party consisted of an old man—his name was Tacaŋhpi Kokipapi, meaning They Are Afraid of His War Club; and a young man,
Witoye, meaning Blue or Bluing or Blue Dye; and Waŋbdiwayape,
meaning Eagle Holding Something in His Mouth; and his father, Nape
Maza, this is Iron Hand. Also, two women and a girl were in the party.

The western people were the real buffalo hunters, whereas at home in Minnesota buffalo were scarce, as that was timber country, but there was a great deal of other kinds of game upon which the people subsisted. Also, in Minnesota, there were many lakes and rivers that furnished fish and turtles.

This happened a long time before the war of 1862. They went out west to the Missouri River on a visiting expedition among the Titoŋwaŋ Indians and had lived there all winter with them. It was getting into the spring when the snow first began to thaw. And at that time, when it would be getting warm weather, they were going to start for their homes in Minnesota. They had seven horses (ponies). Three were loaded with wood and one was loaded with the tent and poles and three were loaded with other goods. Blankets, kettles, ammunition, etc. They were to start out on a warm day when it was pleasant.

One fine morning, the village herald was heard to cry around the village, "The buffalo have reached here! They are so thick that they cover the ground entirely. No room between them." The people of the village did not understand it, but the reason that they had come down this way was that a great blizzard was coming, and the buffalo had come to take refuge in the lee of the woods.

The visitors left the camp with the hunters and crossed the bottomland coming toward the east. The hunt was immediately in progress, and a great many buffalo were killed. As the Santee came across the hunting grounds, a man was butchering a buffalo not far away, and the woman said to her husband, "Go and get a piece of fresh meat for me." So, he went and got a piece of meat and just at that time, he looked around and saw that up in the north, a bad blizzard was approaching. He immediately yelled, "Huhu!" (a cry of alarm). "Look up north—there, a blizzard is coming." As he said this, someone else cried out the same thing, and then another repeated it until it was echoed all over the hunting field. A small, dark cloud low down was just coming up in the north.

As the news was spread among the hunters, they started to make desperate efforts to get home, and some wanted to take the meat with them and hurriedly loaded some on their packhorses. The old man brought the piece of meat back to his wife, and they proceeded to look for a camping place, as they well knew that flight was impossible. It was impossible to seek shelter in a ravine, and it was impossible to return to the village.

Just then, the storm struck with all its fury. They got to the top of a small rise of land and decided to camp right there regardless of the difficulties involved. Setting up a tent was out of the question. Their seven horses or ponies were all loaded with packs of their property. Three were loaded with wood, and one was loaded with the tent and poles, and three were loaded with other goods, blankets, kettles, ammunition, etc. As no time could be spared, they took their knives and cut the packs loose from all the ponies and thus freed them so they could shift for themselves and maybe find shelter in some ravine or a clump of trees.

Setting up the tent was out of the question. They got an old tent off of one of the packhorses and spread it out on the ground, and the whole group got under it. In the middle, they set up a pole in a makeshift way to hold it off the ground a little. There they just sat and waited while the blizzard roared and piled the snow over them. Some lying under the tent unknowingly shifted their positions, but all were under the tent, and the snow drifted over them and also blew in under the tent.

They had no fire and no blankets except what they had on themselves, but as it was into the spring, it was not extremely cold and the snow piling over the tent made it warm under it. They sat under this makeshift shelter for two days and two nights, and on the third day the old man just had to make some kind of a move, although the storm was just as furious as at the start. He lifted the edge of the tent, but the snow was piled so deep on it that it took a lot of digging with his hunting knife before he could get outside.

The minute he got outside, his blanket and shirt that he wore froze stiff and the wind blew through him, too, and made him very cold. The storm was just as bad, although he could see the sun just a little. When he was going back into the tent, his blanket was spread out and frozen stiff, so he could not get it back in the tent but had to leave it to cover up the hole he dug in the snow like a door over it.

When he got inside, he had such a chill and he thought he was going to be sick and even thought he might die. But his wife got out his pipe for him and filled it and lit it for him, and after he had taken a few puffs, the warm smoke seemed to warm him up and he came out alright, and she also found a dry shirt for him to put on.

On the next day, when they thought it was about to break, he went outside again, and the roar of the wind had stopped. So, the old man went outside, and the lady was going out with him. They had on good clothes, but from being inside they were damp. They got outside and the blizzard had stopped, but there was a little snow yet sifting along low down.

They had removed the tent and poles off the packhorses, and they were laying on the ground and had not drifted under at all. So, they prepared to set up a tent and stuck the tent poles in the snow in a circle. They had Indian snow shovels with them, which were made out of wood, smooth like a canoe paddle; only the blade was made wide and curved. With these they began to clear off the snow around the tent.

He started to hunt for the others that were with him. They had all lay down together under the tent, but as they had moved around some, with the wind so bad, it had shoved the others off and they had got outside of the tent. They began digging in the snow and finally came upon the blanket of the girl. They called to her thinking she was dead, but she answered them. She had a blanket of skunk skins which she wore. She was very warm. They say that the skunk skin is very warm. "How is your mother?" they asked her. "Mother died some time ago," she said.

They dug further and found her mother with her hair frozen down to the ground. They dug her out and thought she was dead, but her heart was still beating, so they tried to restore her to life. They powdered up some sweet flag root and washed her with that and she came to. She said, "A man came by here with a gun and stepped on me." He was probably one of the hunters who wandered around there in the storm and stepped on her and did not know it.

Upon looking down on the hunting field, they saw a horseman coming. They thought it was one of the hunters who had got snowed under and had now come out and was coming to see them. They waited for him to come up to them, and finally, seeing that he did not come, they looked closer and saw that it was a man frozen to death on horseback. The hunters were naked. When they went into a hunt, they would throw off their blankets and shirts and wash themselves in snow and start out. In the butchering, the knives would freeze to their hands and they would wash their hands in the snow.

In the *Iapi Oaye* of February 1900, there is a winter count—a year calendar owned by someone named Tate. In that winter count, the year 1850 is called Sicaŋġu Cuwita Ṭapi, that is the Sicaŋġu (band) froze to death. Possibly that refers to the incidents of this story.

> The *Iapi Oaye* (Word Carrier) was a Dakota-language newspaper published by missionaries from 1871 to 1939, first on the Yankton Reservation in South Dakota and then on the Santee Reservation in Nebraska. This article is titled "Waniyetu Yawapi Wan."

Wamnaheza and Paśdayapi

This is what I was taught here at Pejuhutazizi. Dakota recognized two kinds of Indian corn: namely, kohdi and wamnaheza. The former is known as flint corn and the latter as maize. Wamnaheza was the preferred corn. Kohdi is shiny and very hard, and it looks to me like a transparent bead, while wamnaheza is a matte color and was preferred because it was easier to soften.

I am reminded of my mother saying "I can hear that word *maize* in our Dakota word *wamnaheza*," as I can, too, after she pointed it out. As I understand, maize came from Mexico, Central America, or in that general area. So, I suspect when it was brought north that perhaps that name came along with it, with other tribes adopting a similar name for it. I have also noticed other similarity with words from there. For example, Teotihuacán, the ancient city in Mexico where the pyramids are, sounds and means almost the same in Dakota: TiotiWakaŋ—Where God Lives. How interesting it is to discover clues through language. I am so interested in word derivation, and if I were in college yet, I would pursue such a direction.

• • • •

Because the flint corn, or kohdi, has such a hard kernel, it is extra difficult to soften with wood ash. Thus, I was always encouraged to grow

Dekśi Super's wamnaheza in many colors.

wamnaheza. I grew wamnaheza and I was grilled by the local elders of that time, making sure I did not grow kohdi but wamnaheza. Over twenty years ago, when I retired and moved home, I started planting wamnaheza—white corn I got from the Cavenders. But there were also a few colored kernels in there, and because my grandpa Waŋbdiska always had colored corn, I started planting only the colored seed. In about five years, my corn had changed to almost all colored with little white. I liked the blue and red seeds, so I started planting only those seeds, and now I have mainly those colors—beautiful. So, it is easy to manipulate the colors, and I see some names for Indian corn specifying a certain name, but it can all be changed by selective breeding.

• • • •

Grandpa Waŋbdiska used to raise Indian corn and make paśdayapi, our treasured Dakota soup, for our community. "Grandpa, can you make some more of that paśdayapi? That was good." Then, after he died, Elsie Cavender took over the duties and did it until she died. There was a lull in the action until I retired and moved home and took up the charge. Now I am doing it. I am following in my grandfather's footsteps in making paśdayapi and bringing it to community events. I have taught enough people how to do this, so I hope

somebody follows me after I am gone, because I am going to reincarnate here, so the tradition better survive! Paṡdayapi ties us to our
Dakota culture just as wacipi (powwow), siŋkpetawote, tipsiŋna, and
other Dakota foods and medicines. Besides, it tastes so dang good.

Paṡdayapi is made with lyed corn, also called hominy. Hardwood
ashes are a mild form of lye. Regular lye has a pH of 12 to 13, which is
pretty caustic. Now, I have heard of some people using baking soda
in place of ashes. Baking soda has a pH of 8, which is barely a base, as
a pH of 7 is neutral. Hardwood ash has a pH of 9 to 13, a higher level.
So, if one uses baking soda, perhaps it takes longer. Pa means head, or
in this case kernel, ṡdaya means to make bald, thus they make the kernel bald. The goal is to remove the hull of the Indian corn, maize, or
wamnaheza to release the nutrients inside the kernel, namely niacin.

The corn is boiled with the ashes for two to three hours until the
kernels burst open, becoming larger and softer. The other important
step is to rinse the corn and wash out the ashes. The biggest mistake
one can make is not to thoroughly get all the ashes out. And it is quite
an embarrassment when a newbie proudly feeds paṡdayapi to an
esteemed elder and while eating hears a crunch—a chunk of ash left
in, a faux pas extraordinaire. I told this to another student of mine
and she now rinses her corn twice, not taking a chance that she will
be embarrassed by such. But actually, the answer to this dilemma is to
use a flour sifter to eliminate large chunks of ash so that only fine ash
goes through the colander or sieve.

To make paṡdayapi: Soak tipsiŋna for tomorrow's paṡdayapi. Place
one quart of shelled Indian corn in a pot of water. Stir one cup white
hardwood ashes into corn (sift ashes first so dark charcoal is gone).
Soak overnight. Then boil for two to three hours until corn expands
and softens. Rinse corn in colander or sieve to wash out ashes (rinse
one or two cups at a time). After corn is rinsed, place into second pot.
Add water to cover corn. Cut up and add meat (three pounds beef
roast and some beef short ribs). Add vegetables (turnips or prairie
turnips, rutabaga, onion). Add seasoning (salt, pepper, chili powder)
to taste. Add water to cover meat and vegetables. Stir thoroughly.
Cook for one hour, and it's ready to eat. Ho hecetu mitakuyapi—
that's the way it is, my relatives.

• • • •

This I call my Paśdayapi Story even though it is only incidental to the story. There were some Dakota women rinsing their corn in the Mississippi River sometime before the 1851 treaty, since at this time most of Minnesota, at least the southern part, was still Dakota country. However, across the river was Wisconsin Territory and white settlement. From the circumstances, one can determine that these were Mdewakaŋtoŋwaŋ, as Wapahaśa had his village here along the Mississippi River. These women chopped a hole in the ice to rinse the ashes from their corn in the process of making paśdayapi. Over across the river, they could see something but were not sure what it was, but it continued to come toward them. As it came closer, they noticed that this was a white child, who proceeded to come to them and pick up the corn that fell on the ice and eat it. They had no idea where this waśicuŋ boy came from. And after they finished, they were discussing what to do with this boy. Some said that they could not take the boy lest they be charged with stealing him, but the others said he would certainly die if they left him, so one woman took him and raised him as her son. Of course, what name would he have but Waśicuŋ?

He was raised as a Dakota, and when the war came in 1862, he participated and was one of those charged to be hanged. As the story goes, the day they were hanged, an officer came into the wood stockade where the prisoners were held and called out the names to be hanged. Maybe there was more than one man named Waśicuŋ, but when they called that name and no one else answered, he is supposed to have said something on the line of "Okay, I'll go." On the list of those hanged is the name Waśicuŋ, and this is his story. As a postscript: I ran across his trial transcript while looking for some information on my great-grandfather Francois LaBatte's death in 1862. And in that trial record a witness said that he saw this man shoot LaBatte's son. Well, there was no son of Francois killed, just Francois. So, it appears Waśicuŋ was hanged for something that never happened. This is a story from my grandfather Waŋbdiska.

• • • •

An annotated transcript of Waśicuŋ's trial is printed in John Isch's book, *The Dakota Trials*. Isch comes to the same conclusion: no son of Francois LaBatte was killed.

The first time I made paṡdayapi, no one had really taught me—I just remembered what Mom told me. So, I wasn't really sure if I was doing it correctly, until I recognized the beautiful smell which I remember at Grandpa's house, and saw the puffed-up kernels, and then I knew I was doing it the left way.

There are some waṡicuŋ who know about and appreciate paṡdayapi, and by contrast, there are some Dakota who don't because, I assume, they have lost touch with that part of their culture. And so, it is my wish to preserve the growing, harvesting, and processing of the wamnaheza and the making of paṡdayapi. But at the same time, I have concerns about it becoming too popular, where it is exploited like other ethnic foods. I am concerned because I know they will make shortcuts by using canned hominy instead of our traditional methods. I know that the canned hominy is a poor substitute for the original. And I am afraid this will become known as paṡdayapi and the original will be lost.

The Jewish people have chicken soup as their medicine—Jewish penicillin. When I cook paṡdayapi, I remember an admonition from my mother to not feed paṡdayapi to sick people. I never asked her why, but I mentioned that to some other elders here and they agreed—they had heard that from their elder relatives, too. Maybe when you have the flu or a cold, you lose your appetite and eating paṡdayapi might make you throw up. Just my opinion.

• • • •

My mother was rather funny sometimes, and when I think about her, I smile. Twenty-some years ago when I started to plant wamnaheza to make paṡdayapi, I asked her what I should charge for a quart. She told me this ridiculously low price—probably just apt in Grandpa's days—but I told her the price people were charging for waskuya, dried sweet corn. I told what I thought I should get, and she said, "Well, if you can get that price . . ."

Some years ago, I was talking with a local waṡicuŋ farmer and told him about my wamnaheza—specifically, the price I got for a quart of dried corn. I could see him making calculations: "How many quarts in a bushel? Oh my God, I could be a millionaire." But I told him you can't use chemical fertilizer or weed killer. And you have to cultivate the corn during the growing season. I could see him slump. "That's too much work. I want to fish all summer, not work."

One year, I didn't go around peddling my corn—just waited for people to call. But a couple of years ago, I would load up my corn in quart baggies and put them in the trunk and head to Sisseton. They were and are good customers of mine because they still remember how good paśdayapi tastes. One lady who shall remain unnamed came to my trunk to buy corn and said, "Oh my gosh, it's been a long time since I bought something in baggies from somebody's trunk." Don't worry; I shall never disclose who you are. Oh, by the way, I didn't even know who she was.

• • • •

A group from the University of Minnesota Morris came to see me to learn about Indian corn and processing into soup. U of M Morris, the former boarding school for Indians. Dad's siblings went to school there. Dad went to Flandreau, and at that time Flandreau Indian School had its own farm and animals. Dad said you worked half the day on the farm and went to school the other half. They taught farming, among other subjects, so I find it ironic that now this school sends its students to learn from an Indian how to raise Indian corn.

• • • •

The Morris Industrial School for Indians was operated from 1887 to 1909, first by the Catholic Sisters of Mercy and then by the federal government. As at other boarding schools, students spent half a day in classes and half learning "industries"—field work, laundry, cooking, and sewing. Its federal superintendent refused to send students home for vacations and argued with his Native staff, who found his behavior unchristian; he was also accused of raping two students. In 1910, it became an agricultural high school, part of the University of Minnesota, with the stipulation that Native students be admitted free of charge. In 1960, it became the University of Minnesota–Morris, and Native students still attend tuition-free.

Dekši Super cultivating.

Gardening is more than just planting and waiting for the harvest.
It is a lot of tender care to make the best environment for the plants
to prosper. And then stepping back to let the plants do their magic
of making food. Sounds a little like life, yes? Except there is no one
there to block you from getting to the garden.

   When Dad and I farmed, we planted field corn, and with this corn,
it had roots out of the ground which help support the stalk. If you
covered those roots, it would develop new ones above the ground.
My Indian corn does not have that extra support, so I am always wary
when the winds come up and I hope the plants don't get blown down
like they did one year.

   One year, I was not motivated to garden. I can't remember what
was going on in my life. Nonetheless, I planted corn—probably just
to keep my crop rotation in place. But I neglected my corn; not even
once did I cultivate it or check on it. Come fall, I decided to look, and

yes, it was covered in weeds. My corn must have taken pity on me, though, because though production was down, I harvested enough for some paṡdayapi and for seed for the next year. I never again neglected my corn.

My mom taught me to plant my Indian corn by poking a hole in the ground every eight inches or so and dropping in three or four seeds, so that if one seed does not germinate, others will. This takes me all day, or at least all afternoon, to plant. Some years, I use a planter, but I notice it skips seed, so that I have small stretches with no plants. Depending on the soil, I decide each year if I'm going to cultivate by hand or with a tractor and cultivator. Either way, I farm just like my dad and I did in the '50s and '60s. No genetically modified corn. No chemicals—horse manure and cultivating. Glad this isn't for making a living but just for fun.

When the corn grows beyond knee high, closer to thigh high, cultivating would probably injure the plants. So it's on its own. Maybe when we caretake we do more damage than helping. The tall corn plants will take care of some of the weeds themselves by shading them out.

One year, my corn was getting too tall to cultivate, but I was pulling weeds, nonetheless. I have noticed how cunning, tricky the weeds are, and I suppose Mother Nature. There is a weed that that looks like a corn plant and always places itself in the row next to a corn plant, hoping to camouflage itself so I won't pull. I have to look twice before I make a decision. That's how the weeds adapt to survive. Here's a toast to the weeds and Mother Nature.

• • • •

My wamnaheza sways in the wind like Fancy Dancers, with the tassels looking like the roach feathers and the leaves looking like the top bustle feathers.

• • • •

Ever since I saw that painting by Seth Eastman of Indian women on a platform in a cornfield scaring away the birds, I questioned that occurrence. I had the same discussion with my friend Beth. All the times that I farmed, and now when I grow my Indian corn, I have never had birds eat my corn. The rascals have always been racoons and deer. So, what is the difference between today and during the 1830s and 1840s, the time of Eastman, that birds were the pests of that era? I can't imagine Eastman painting something that was not true. Or did he believe he had gullible art patrons of his day who would not question?

• • • •

Oh, the broth is heavenly. This is the reason I will reincarnate as a Dakota. All you people who I taught how to make paśdayapi, remember to pass it on to the next generation, so I will be able to partake of this delicious victual in my next life.

Waskuya

Some years ago, my aunt Harriet used the word śtuŋka, meaning unripe, to explain our way of making waskuya, dried sweet corn. She explained that you made waskuya when the sweet corn was in that stage, śtuŋka—the milky stage. She said one used that spoon to get the kernel off whole, so that the milk in the corn stays intact—that is the sweet part of the sweet corn—instead of being in a hurry and just cutting the kernels off with a knife. At the time, I did not know the Lakota word for the same process: making waśtuŋkala. Now I understand that word well.

Wahpe

My grandpa mentioned that there was a certain type or brand of tea that those living here who had earlier fled to Canada became accustomed to and liked but was rarely available here. Grandpa said when it was, those people would buy out the entire lot of tea in one day. So, Great-Grandmother Susbe was not the only one here with the Canadian experience, secece. Grandpa did not mention names, but it would be interesting to find out who the others were, and if their descendants had stories to tell also of their experiences of that era and in Canada.

Caŋpa

There used to be a big rock in our pasture. As kids we helped Mom make caŋpa wojapi. We kids used to pound the chokecherries for my mom on this big rock we had, and she took it to make caŋpa wojapi for immediate consumption, but later she canned, also. We were always told to make sure that we pound them good, so no pits remained. I later found out the pits contained cyanide gas, but it must have dissipated when crushed, as we obviously never died from cyanide poisoning. This was one of the few fruits we had during winter. This rock now sits in my sister Sarah's yard. Glad they saved it. Must have been moved when her driveway was put in. Perhaps only an Indian can get nostalgic over a rock. Our mitakuye.

Pejuta

No better place to be than home when sick. Ho ahpe—I have a sore throat. But the literal translation is, the voice is gone. It is one of those idioms which means, in other words, to have a sore throat. I received some native plants from the tribe. I planted my siŋkpetawote (muskrat's food) in a wet area I found, so it should prosper in the wetlands. Its English name is sweet flag. Many also call it bitter root, but that can apply to a whole host of root medicines. This medicine is used for sore throats.

• • • •

Oh, I remember last night, "dreaming" or not? But I smelled caŋśaśa, the kind of my youth, that good-smelling stuff, not the hybridized red osier dogwood, which has no smell. I am sure it came from the spirit world, so Grandpa, Dad, or whoever brought it, thank you.

• • • •

In 1918, the world was swept by a deadly flu, often called the Spanish flu. My dad's brother Solon LaBatte died from this. My mother said her grandmother Susbe saged her and her sisters every night. This, she assured us, is why they did not get the flu. Now I have read lately that there is evidence that pejiȟota kills germs in the air. Taśina-susbecawiŋ, you are proven true.

One year, I was out in Montana when I spied a beautiful patch of pejiȟota, or sage, in the gravel alongside this country road—it smelled so strong and good. I transplanted a few plants when I got home in my rich, fertile black soil, but it did not prosper and eventually died out. But the next year, it showed up alongside my driveway, where I had placed a foot of gravel as my base material under the concrete. Now these new plants had to have come from seed of this sage, as there were no other sage nearby. It makes one wonder if plants have a consciousness of their own where they want to live and take appropriate action to find the right environment to grow. That was a good twenty years ago, and they continue to grow along my driveway.

• • • •

Okay, another of Dad's stories comes to mind. (He must be near.) Dad told of the time he was a child with a persistent earache and for days constantly crying. It was winter. His mother went to get a medicine man, who heated up the rocks outside. When they were glowing, he brought them inside in a basin and made a makeshift sweat with blankets and chairs—bringing the inipi inside, so to speak. The man took him inside the sweat and put some medicine on the rocks, and fortunately his earache went away almost immediately. So, Dad

The young Walter La-Batte Sr., about 1904.

always recognized sweats as a place for physical healing, too, as well as a place to pray. My uncle Sidney LaBatte, Dad's older brother, also told me of his healing from a medicine man. In those days, they must have relied on Indian doctoring rather than a white-man doctor, if any existed at that time on the Sisseton Reservation. Dad did not know what kind of medicine he used but was grateful for the relief from the earache.

Storytelling

I had a long conversation with an elder from Sisseton, and he shared a couple stories. I told him yes, that I remember stories from my youth, but I told him if someone asked me when I was forty, I would have said, "No, I don't know any stories." But when I reached a certain age, they started falling out of my head. He said that it was the same with him, that he initially didn't know that he knew these stories. He knew my grandfather Waŋbdiska and shared that after supper, Grandpa got out his drum and they sang some old, old songs that he wished he could have recorded. I didn't know Grandpa was a singer. He said, too, he was incredulous when his dad told him Grandpa was a wašicuŋ, since Grandpa talked nothing but Dakota. One time, an elder here who was fluent in Dakota admitted that she sometimes consulted Grandpa on how to say something in Dakota.

• • • •

For some reason I have been thinking of all the Uŋktomi stories I heard as a kid. I could always reckon them with Minnesota because they talk about lakes, sloughs, and in one they mention names of the trees—all native to here in Minnesota. So, I assume these are ancient stories told when all the "Sioux" lived in Minnesota. I can hardly think of placing these stories in West River (i.e., on the high dry plains). So, if the Lakota tell Uŋktomi stories, does it harken back to life in Minnesota for them?

There are a number of written accounts of some of the Uŋktomi stories which I have read. But there are two stories that deal with the taboo subject of sex—perhaps not so much then, but by today's standards, which is likely due to religious influences. It is only later that I understood the reason for the telling of these stories. In my case, it was told to me by my dad to assess if I was old enough to be told about the birds and the bees. I know only bits and pieces of the story told to young girls for the same purpose. The boy story is the one where Uŋktomi comes to a lake and hears laughter and water splashing and looks across the lake and sees beautiful young Dakota girls swimming and bathing naked. If you want to know more, you can look it up for yourself.

And there's that well-known Uŋktomi story of the ducks, where the teal duck opens his eyes and catches Uŋktomi up to his bad deeds, and Uŋktomi gives him red eyes. My mom would say we would get red eyes if we saw something we were not supposed to see—for example, if you walked into the bathroom and saw your sister unclothed, she would say you are going to get red eyes.

Dakota Caże

Who were you named after? A favorite uncle, grandpa, aunt, etc.? I was named after a cartoon character, or so my mom tells the story. Not my real name—a little on that later on—but Super. As the story goes, I was crawling on the floor real quickly and came to a chair and pulled myself up. My uncle Snook, aka Fred Blue, saw this and said, "Oh, you're a real Superman." The name stuck and just shortened to Super.

Dad told me how he got his name. His dad, Philip LaBatte, was friendly with the Indian agent or some employee of such at the Sisseton Agency by the name of Walter Allen. Thus, my dad got the name of Walter Allen LaBatte. I ran into a woman in the Cities twenty years ago whose maiden name was Allen. I told her that story and she said that was her relative, a grandfather or great-grandfather. Now there have been four of us LaBatte Juniors. Three of them died before their dads. That got me thinking about how Dad lived to ninety-five.

Dakota caże bduha k'a tuŋkaŋśidaŋ mitawa he mak'u. Waŋbdiska he eciyapi do. Waśicuŋhdinaźin de Dakota caże mitawa. My grandpa Waŋbdiska gave me my Indian name of Spirit Returns, which was my paternal grandfather Philip LaBatte's name. In reference to waśicuŋ in my Dakota name—a Sisitoŋwaŋ relative refers to it with the Sisitoŋwaŋ diminutive ending *na*, as in waśicuŋna. My maternal grandfather, who gave it to me, spoke the Isaŋati dialect, so dropped the diminutive ending. This name giving was done when I was just a child and I don't remember it, but as I got older, Grandpa always translated wašicuŋ as spirit, and not as white man. It took me years to figure it out. I found out that there is a spirit (guardian) that accompanies you during your lifetime, and this definition of wašicuŋ was applied to that before it was applied to white people. It has something to do with those rock spirits in the sweat, the sicuŋ or šicuŋ—I have heard it referred to as both. After some research, I found out that initially this meant spirit guide, that one that's with you through your life to guide and help you. I have on numerous occasions experienced that help and I no longer call it just coincidence—where circumstances mysteriously align themselves for your benefit. I believe everyone has the same help available if you don't drive it away with drink or drugs. Now that is what I know about the subject, but I am sure someone has a different story of wašicuŋ. Ho hecetu mitakuyapi. Hau de miye do Wašicuŋhdinažiŋ emakiyapi do. Spirit Returns.

• • • •

Wašicuŋhdinažiŋ or Philip LaBatte, Dekši Super's grandfather and namesake.

I find it interesting that Grandpa Waŋbdiska had five daughters, so he used up all the female birth order names: Stella was Winona, Evelyn was Hapaŋ, Harriet was Hapstiŋna, Cerisse was Waŋske, and my mother was the youngest with Wihake. And I heard them called such in my young days.

· · · ·

I went to Tahaŋsi Marlow's wake, and I remember his mother who later became known an Angie, but we all knew her as Angelique when the family lived here. I am always amazed at apparent coincidences or synchronicities, as follows. Back in the '70s, I did my family history, and I discovered that my great-great-grandmother's name was Angelique LaBatte. She was the daughter of Wapahaśa I—the first Wapahaśa—and married my great-great-grandfather, Michel LaBatte. I asked Marlow's grandfather, Archie LaBatte, why he named his daughter Angelique, and he said that he didn't, that his wife, Pearl, named her that. Neither Archie nor Pearl knew that name was in our family tree. Now that would not be so astounding were the name more common, but you must admit Angelique is not a very common name. So, the mysteries of life continue to amaze me.

Dakota Iapi

The Sisitoŋwaŋ often camped with and hunted buffalo with the Ihaŋktoŋwaŋna band called the Pabaksa (Cut Heads). And after the establishment of the Fort Totten Reservation, some of the Pabaksa settled in with the Sisitoŋwaŋ and Waȟpetoŋwaŋ there. To my way of thinking, this allied friendship must have had an influence on the Sisitoŋwaŋ speech, where the use of the *n* became prevalent in many Dakota words. The use of hokśina instead of the usual hokśidaŋ, tuŋkaŋśina for tuŋkaŋśidaŋ, bde for mde are just a few of the examples. As I have mentioned before, I was raised in a family where both dialects were spoken, though both my parents were Sisitoŋwaŋ Waȟpetoŋwaŋ. My mother was raised by her Isaŋati grandmother, as her mother died shortly after she was born. Dad often mentioned the difference in the two dialects. And today there are few Mdewakaŋtoŋwaŋ speakers left, so many believe that Sisitoŋwaŋ is or was the only Dakota dialect. There exists a film clip from Lower Sioux circa

Sometime between 1862 and his death in 1892, Tiwakaŋ (Gabriel
Renville) recorded his memories, in Dakota. They were translated
into English by Samuel J. Brown and Thomas A. Robertson (see
page 152) and published by the Minnesota Historical Society in
1905 as "A Sioux Narrative of the Outbreak in 1862, and of Sibley's
Expedition in 1863."

1960s with three Dakota male elders. In that clip the word Mdewakaŋtoŋwaŋ is easily heard—distinct from the Sisitoŋwaŋ pronunciation of Bdewakaŋtoŋwaŋ.

I should like to reread Tiwakaŋ's (Gabriel Renville's) Narrative to
see if I can get a hint of the *n* dialect. Twenty to thirty years ago, when
I read it last, I never paid much attention to that. Though what stands
out in my memory was that he used no punctuation, so it was sort of
difficult to read.

By the way, to my way of thinking (my grandfather's words), the
Isaŋati are the same people as the (B)Mdewakaŋtoŋwaŋ, and the
words are used interchangeably. Also, I often hear Lakota refer to
all Dakota as Isaŋati. However, Isaŋati refers only to one of the four
bands. Ho hecetu.

The reason I bring up this subject is that I continue to hear the
false accusation that Riggs in his dictionary turned all the bde words
to mde as in the above case. Quite the contrary—in his introduction
he makes it clear that this is the Mdewakaŋtoŋwaŋ dialect, and he
even mentions that the Sisitoŋwaŋ differs in some cases, but that
does not affect the usefulness of this dictionary.

• • • •

I remember Dad sitting at the kitchen table with his Bible, writing
down his sermon in Dakota on Saturday afternoon. Two Sundays
a month, the church elders did the church service, as we shared a
minister with First Presbyterian in Flandreau. At that time, this was
the regular practice—for the other elders to deliver their sermon
in Dakota, as all in that generation wrote, read, and spoke Dakota.
There was at that time a plethora of written Dakota material. I have
family letters written in Dakota, as do other families; that is how

they communicated with far-off relatives and Dakota friends. Written Dakota continues to exist. For example, the *Iapi Oaye*, a Dakota newspaper, is still available. In it are Dakota story articles, news from correspondents about what is happening in the Dakota churches—all written in Dakota. In Riggs's grammar book are stories, legends, etc., written by Dakota writers of that era. What a teaching material available to teach Dakota! One can study sentence structure, grammar, vocabulary, how to write and communicate in Dakota. What a treasure trove of material to learn Dakota.

> Stephen Riggs's *Dakota Grammar with Texts and Ethnography* was published in 1852 by the Smithsonian with the support of the Minnesota Historical Society and reprinted by the society in 2004.

• • • •

I wonder where my parents learned to become literate in Dakota. I remember one time I came home from school and was reciting and memorizing the German alphabet when Dad heard me and said it was almost the same as the Dakota alphabet. He proceeded to recite the Dakota alphabet and it was pretty similar in that the vowels (*a, e, i, o, u*) were pronounced the same and most consonants also were alike with few exceptions. Would a fluent speaker without studying the language necessarily be able to recite the alphabet, without having studied the language? Maybe, but I think not.

• • • •

In my parents' generation, they were of course all fluent in Dakota and were all able to read and write in Dakota. I suppose that was due to the church, where one learned to read the Bible in Dakota, preach in Dakota, and sing our Dakota odowaŋpi. They probably thought that was an asset to Dakota culture, to be able to communicate over distances by letter. I don't believe they thought of that as colonization or being wašicuŋ, or that they insisted that Dakota was an oral language only. Something happened after that, whereby fluent speakers don't want to read and write, using the excuse it is wašicuŋ. But really, I believe it's covering up a shame that they never learned to read and write Dakota. Grammar is the book of rules of how a language is put together, which is also ignored in a lot of cases. Just as in English we don't think about grammar because those rules are embedded in our brain, so we speak without referring to that. But that is not the case with new learners, so I believe it is beneficial to teach, also.

I suppose with today's technology, one can transmit knowledge to one's descendants orally in Dakota. But I am thoroughly grateful to my grandfather and great-grandfather for learning that new wašicuŋ technology of writing and leaving written documentations of their experiences—Great-Grandfather for preserving his experiences during 1862, and Grandfather for telling us of his rather quaint experience of first encounter with a gas cookstove in a letter to his daughter in the 1950s. There were many other Dakota who learned to write in Dakota and have left us important information via stories and experiences. I know there are Dakota today who believe in only a spoken Dakota, but I think otherwise.

· · · ·

Sometimes the original meanings of Dakota words, phrases, or names are forgotten over time, but the name remains. Here are two such examples, though we know of many. Years ago, my mother asked if Mazaśa should be Mazaś'a. That is, instead of Red Iron, perhaps Iron Making a Noise. It is sometimes translated as Sounding Iron. Unless the story of a name is kept, the original meaning can be lost. I need to ensure that the proper translation of my Dakota name survives. In my name is the word wašicuŋ, meaning spirit instead of white man. And translating it as spirit makes so much more sense in the context of the entire name.

Sometimes there are words in Dakota which are so similar but with different meanings, and so it takes a good ear to distinguish—or an understanding of the context to comprehend. I heard this woman from Standing Rock refer to her band as Wiciyena, but I heard Wiciyaŋna, meaning young girl. I was perplexed why they called their band Little Girl, as I had never heard that term before. Only with a little research did I find out Wiciyena is how the Yanktonnai refer to themselves.

· · · ·

Grandpa Fred translated for the government and the courts, especially in probate heirship cases to ascertain who were eligible to share
in a person's estate—mainly land allotments, I assume. The court
needed to determine, for example, that the deceased was the ate,
father, of this person claiming to be a relative. Often these Dakota
familial terms were different from wašicuŋ terms, and this had an ob-
vious effect on who inherited from the person's estate. Grandpa wrote
about questioning this person, to determine huŋka relationships from
the other, as he said it was often confusing to the court.

• • • •

When I was young, there was a kuŋśi by the name of Elizabeth
Blue, probably born circa 1880, as she remembered meeting Sitting
Bull as a child. She was much older than my parents, probably a
generation before. She had this unique greeting in Dakota, "Hau
cucu." I am pretty sure it was hau instead of haŋ, but I could be
wrong. We all just accepted it as her unique saying and never asked
why—meaning we accepted it and didn't criticize her for using
men's language. I once asked my cousin Dean Blue about it, and he
never knew, either.

"Caŋdi mak'u pe," an entreaty, meaning please give me a cigarette.
My mother said that is not so demanding and harsh, and she also said
that it was permissible for males to use that form. That made so much
sense to me in this case, as why would a beggar demand for a cigarette
(i.e., Caŋdi mak'u wo—Give me a cigarette)?

In my youth here at Pejuhutazizi, "Ho eca!" was a perfectly good
interjection, meaning disagreement or dissent response, for both men
and women. Now I hear from others that that is woman speech and
kind of derision and am ridiculed when I use that word.

• • • •

Another word I remember hearing a lot in my youth was icazo, meaning to charge a purchase or buy on credit, but I don't hear it used
much anymore. In my youth, I always took that as a negative conno-
tation, something not to do—but of course, America is built on credit,
otherwise there would be no use for banks. Given all that, I thought if
I don't have the money for it, I will not buy it, and that has served me

well. I think of the 1851 Treaty of Traverse des Sioux, whereby traders got a good share of our treaty money because of icazo. In reference to the "trader's papers," these were the documents our Dakota people were tricked into signing that gave so much of our money to the fur traders who claimed debts. I remember finding them in my research of family history back in the 1970s. It was a list of how much money each trader received from the 1851 treaty. And lo and behold, I found my great-grandfather's name, Francois LaBatte, a half-Dakota, half-French fur trader. He married a full-blood, Mary Ironshield—I can't find her Dakota name, other than Wahacaŋka Maza (Iron Shield). Francois was on the bottom of the list with the least amount of money received, at $500, not an insignificant amount in 1851. However, the other traders received much more. If I remember correctly, Henry Sibley received over $66,000. Sececa there was no accounting of the accuracy of the bills submitted; the government just paid what was submitted. (Sececa—it seems—and naceca—probably—are so similar they can be used interchangeably, sececa.)

· · · ·

My mother said, "Super, I know you dance all over Dakota country, and I want you to find out if those Dakota know this saying: 'Waŋna sicaŋ wayaŋkapi.'" An idiom is a saying that cannot be deciphered from the exact translation of its words. This is one such case, as the word-for-word translation is "The thighs are visible" or "They can see the thighs." My mother said it means something like "Their true colors are coming out" or "They can't fool the people anymore." This was used to refer to those who have such lofty speech but with a hidden agenda (e.g., politicians, salesmen). It finally comes out, and the people are fooled no more.

I am trying to reintroduce the Dakota word for excellent, ayuco, now shortened to just co. Thanks, Mom, for enlightening me all those years ago when neither one of us had heard of the word "co," but you figured it out.

When I was young, I used to hang around Dad and Uncle Snook when they were working on a project—maybe a wiring project or carpenter project. And sometimes they would run into a problem and then try different solutions. When one of them came upon the correct action, the other would say in Dakota, "A he a do!" I understood that to mean "That's the right way," or maybe "You got it." I don't know if I spelled it correctly or even if I remember it as such, but I find myself saying the same thing to myself when I have a eureka moment.

A word I heard not too long ago from my youth is witkotkoka. It means foolish, crazy, misbehaving. In that word is the word witko, often used to mean drunk. So, before 1986, I was often witkotkoka, and that is the word I heard often back then.

Wahdeca is a Dakota word Mother told me about years ago that meant a certain sensation, an ache, a pain, that a mother gets in her chest if one of her children is in distress in a far-off place. Considering that we boys were always kind of witkotkoka in our youth, my mom must have felt like she was having a heart attack. There are so many instances that seem to be relegated to Pejuhutazizi only, perhaps because we were always so isolated from other Dakota. The word refers to a mother's intuition, and I was wondering if there is a similar word for a male's intuition. Some years ago, I went on a selling trip out west peddling my brain-tanned hides again with my then wife, Dawn. Of course, this was before cell phones. We were on our way back, and Dawn asked me if we were going to stop in Granite Falls or Pejuhutazizi before going to St. Paul, as we most often would have done. I told her no but didn't explain why. I was feeling a great dread concerning home, and I just wanted to avoid it. I was afraid of hearing about the death of a relative, even perhaps of a parent. So, nearly as soon as we got home to St. Paul, Mom called with the news that my uncle Fred Blue had died, and that they already had his funeral. Oh, man, I felt terrible, but even if we had stopped, it was still too late. I immediately understood the great *dread*.

A Presbyterian minister gave a sermon once about humankind's tendency toward differences rather than unity, the thinking being, my way is better. I was raised in the Dakota Presbyterian Church, where we refer to God as Wakaŋtaŋka—the Great Spirit. Recently, some guy reminded me that "Wakaŋtaŋka is a Christian name, and we traditionalists use Tuŋkaṡila—Grandfather." I told him, "Yes, I know that, but that is the way I was raised." I kind of doubt God gives a care whether you call her Wakaŋtaŋka, Tuŋkaŋṡila, Tuŋkaŋṡidaŋ, Allah, the Creator, or whatever—the one with no gender.

Traditional Brain Tanning

Each spring I hold class for elementary students at the state park on brain tanning, and I have a deer hide stretched. I am always asked if I shot this deer. I always tell them no and tell this story.

Some thirty or forty years ago, I was hunting with my two nephews. They drove this piece of woods and I waited on the end to shoot any deer that came out. While they were driving the woods, I could hear shots, *pow, pow, pow*. So, I knew there was a deer coming, I was at the ready. Out came a doe, and I could see she had been hit. Instead of running away from me, she ran to me. She fell at my feet and made an awful groan or moan noise. My first reaction or instinct was to save her life. I knelt down and felt a deep sadness and almost cried. I regained my composure by the time my nephews came, but that was the last time I hunted. I know most Indians put down tobacco and thanks at the kill site, but I went a step further and quit participating in the kill. I know I am a hypocrite in that I still eat meat and I make buckskin from their skin. Maybe in my next incarnation I will be a vegetarian. "No, Mama, I don't want that meat. Bring peas, carrots, brussels sprouts, and potatoes." "But Super"—for some reason I will

Dekši Super teaching a class at Upper Sioux State Park, 2010.

still be called Super—"you need protein." "Well then, bring me beans, tofu, and peanuts."

. . . .

Again, in my youth when we hunted deer, there were always a lot of hides going to waste. I remember asking my tahaŋ, brother-in-law, if he knew how to tan those hides—he being from Twin Buttes on the Fort Berthold Reservation, I was sure he knew, but he did not. I would take some of those hides and make rawhide to repair horse gear. But I never thought to ask Dad if he knew how. It wasn't until I was in my late thirties that I asked him, quite sure he did not know how. I remember distinctly what he said: "Sure, I used to help my mother make buckskin." That was how I learned to make Indian-tan buckskin.

. . . .

I decided to have my brain-tanning apprentices make their own wahiŋkte and metal scraper blades. The wahiŋkte is a metal blade attached to an elk antler. I sent away for some elk antler for the wahiŋktes. I was just going to wing it, but it is better for me and the apprentices when I am organized.

. . . .

Using a wahiŋkte to flesh a hide.

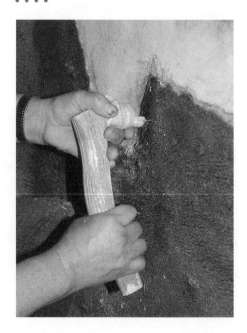

A second fleshing, or taking the membrane off the flesh side, is required. This is as important as taking the hair off along with the epidermis, the top layer of skin. If you all remember in your biology class, you learned that the skin was comprised of three layers: the epidermis, the dermal layer, and the hypodermis. In the process of making Indian tan, the two outer layers must be removed so that the brain solution can penetrate the skin and soften. When the membrane has been removed, it is nearly uniformly white. Removing the hypodermis is a fairly easy job, if one has a sharp scraper.

• • • •

When I'm doing a lot of tanning, I'll have a scraped hide soaking in the laundry tub while I get a hide stretched and ready to dry. The next day, I'll brain the one that was soaking. The day after that, I'll soften it, and then the one stretched should be ready to scrape.

For braining the hide, I soak it in a mixture of pork brains and hot water that I fix up in the blender—it looks like a strawberry malt. I'll force the brain solution through the hide and wring it out, then put it back in the solution again and wring out a couple more times. Then I'll either refrigerate it or continue on to soften the hide, working it by hand until it's thoroughly dry, retaining its softness.

By squeezing and forcing the brain water through the hide, I am getting the brain into the hide. I don't think it is adequate to just let it soak. I watch and feel for the subtle changes that the hide is going through while being brained (a new verb being coined). The hide gets stretchy and gets thicker as it absorbs the brain. Areas of the hide that seem compact and have no stretch need more manipulation to get brain into them.

While I am braining hides, I am waiting for that aha moment where I know the hide is brained well enough. Then I can use that Dakota phrase I often heard my dad and uncle use when they were working on something with little success and finally it came together and succeeded: "A he a do!"

When I get to the stage where I'm softening the hide by hand, I have a quarter-inch cable strung up in the basement, and I pull the hide over it, generating friction (heat) to dry and soften.

• • • •

There is a certain point where the wet rawhide turns into buckskin, though it's still a bit damp and not thoroughly buckskin. But that is an amazing transformation to experience. It is quite satisfying to know that if I continue on this arduous journey, I will end up with a beautiful product. I wish I knew a more scientific reason for what's happening. I wish I could get a microscopic look at a hide before braining and after, to see what is happening.

But still, making buckskin is more art than science. A scientific experiment is always replicable—if you do the same steps the same way, you will always get the same result. That's not the same with art. One can do all the steps the same and not get the same product. This is not unlike the process of making buckskin. There are so many variables that can sabotage your efforts. You may do all the same steps and get beautiful results, or mediocre results, or it may turn into a learning process. One might think "Ah, this hide is not good," but after softening, it's the best hide. Or the opposite—a hide you think is good doesn't turn out. The learning process is finding out what went wrong: Did I not scrape sufficiently, or did I scrape too much so that I weakened the hide? Did I not brain enough? Did I not work the hide enough to soften?

A true artist accepts these uncertainties, in fact kind of welcomes them, for if it were otherwise, it would be like working in a factory.

• • • •

A little info on takaŋ—the backstrap sinew. I have only taken it off a deer, but other animals, such as buffalo and cows, also have it. Takaŋ is the tendon which runs from the hip on both sides of the back to the front legs. It sits on top of the loin and is flat with strings in it. You can see it on certain cuts of meat. I'm sure you have seen it but didn't know it. I take a butter knife and work it under the takaŋ and work it loose—this is not very difficult. I clean it good and let it dry. After it has been dried, you can crunch it and pull the threads off. I sometimes use it to sew up holes in my brain tan, and because it is part of the deer, the hole kind of disappears—you can't see the hole anymore.

• • • •

Some twenty or more years ago, I went to powwow at Browning, Montana, and their grand entry was brought in by the chiefs with bonnets and white buckskin outfits. Man, they looked sharp with the white buckskin. I rarely get calls for the white hide; mostly everybody likes smoked, as it is more durable. But the white looks good for ceremonial.

• • • •

I am so happy and satisfied when I have successfully taken my students through the last step of making Indian-tan buckskin—that is, the smoking of six hides. I hope they all continue making buckskin.

The excitement of opening up a smoked hide to see what it looks like is the same excitement as when I am braiding corn and I get to open the corn to see what color and beauty is inside. Other cultures, other people have come up with different methods of making buckskin or leather. Some use tannins from the bark of the oak tree and other chemicals to soften skins. I am often asked how we came up with using brains for the job; I have no idea why it works. Sometimes I hear of a mythical story of how we learned certain things, but I have heard of no such story for this. I find it improbable, though, that it was just happenstance that brain material was dropped on a hide and it miraculously softened.

• • • •

The only thing I do different from Dad's instructions about making buckskin is that I smoke my hides different. I fold my hide in half and sew it up and leave the bottom open. I hang this above a fire (I use a burn barrel) with rope and then let the smoke come up. Dad said his mother, Sagadaśiŋ, smoked her hides in a sweat lodge. She either laid them on the frame or hung them from the frame and started a fire in the pit, I suspect. I didn't ask for details because I must have assumed it would not work for me. In retrospect, I should have asked for complete details; I always felt Dad wanted me to smoke hides the way Grandma did.

This mention of a sweat lodge in the early 1900s brings up a whole bunch of questions as to the oft-heard statement that traditional Indian spiritual practices were illegal until the 1970s. Why not at Sisseton, then? Dad never hinted that their sweat lodge was illegal, and it was practiced openly. My grandmother's house was at the agency in sight of all the government officials. Perhaps it was the federal law, but

The Oceti Śakowiŋ (Seven Council Fires) are the people whom the whites first called the Great Sioux Nation. The members include the four bands of Dakota (Mdewakaŋtoŋwaŋ, Waȟpekute, Sisitoŋwaŋ, and Waȟpetoŋwaŋ), as well as the Ihaŋktoŋwaŋ, Ihaŋktoŋwaŋna, and Tituŋwaŋ (Lakota). After the US–Dakota War of 1862, the Dakota bands were forced out of their homes in Minnesota and widely dispersed through Canada, North and South Dakota, Montana, and Nebraska. This is the diaspora Dekśi Super refers to. A few Dakota were permitted to remain in Minnesota; later, some Dakota returned to their homeland, despite the Dakota Removal Act.

they didn't enforce it. But can you imagine today having to go into the woods so the "culture police" don't see you? "That's a sacred place, not for secular activities." The culture police must not have been in existence in my grandmother's days.

We may all call ourselves human; we may all call ourselves American Indians or alternative words; we may all call ourselves belonging to the Oceti Śakowiŋ; we may all call ourselves Dakota. But we don't all have the same belief systems; we don't all follow the same protocols; we don't all have the same cultural, spiritual ways. So, it takes a small mind to criticize others for not following your ways. After the diaspora, we were all raised in unique geographic areas, different eras; were taught different ways from our parents. The answer is acceptance, in order to maintain peace and serenity.

• • • •

I have been pondering if it is normal or natural to procrastinate when wanting to learn from our elders. For example, the thought "Oh, he'll still be around" or "I can wait to ask her." When it came to learning how to make buckskin, for me, it was pure chance that I asked Dad if he knew how. I was expecting a no answer but am so glad I asked the question. This is also said in gratitude for my apprentices who step up to the plate and enthusiastically learn what I have to offer. Wopida taŋka, apprentices. So, let's continue what my dad taught all those years ago. Ho hecetu mitakuyapi.

Beading and Moccasin Making

I have a pair of my paternal grandmother Sagadaśiŋ's (Sarah Renville LaBatte's) soft-sole moccasins. Though she was Sisitoŋwaŋ, this style is often called Isaŋati style. I could never figure out how to make them. I asked my mother if she knew how, and she said, "Yes, I used to help Grandma make them." She told me to come up and she would show me. Unfortunately, I never did before she died. A lesson to the young! I found a pattern for the soft-sole moccasins, not exactly like them, but close enough so that I could reproduce Grandmother's. The cuffs are wider on hers than the pattern, and she added the beaded front tongue, while the pattern doesn't have this. I decided to make some—and to learn how to bead flowers.

I don't know what Kuŋśi had in mind when she beaded these floral moccasins—whether she had a particular flower in mind or just used her creativity in making "stylized" flowers. I kind of copied her flowers to learn technique, knowing that I could later use my own creativity in coming up with designs, which maybe she did, too. Perhaps we overthink people's designs and assign meanings that the artist never meant in the first place. When an artist assigns meaning to a design, almost surely the culture police will dispute that to say, "No, that means this."

I am so used to symmetry in my moccasins in that I put the same design on both sides of my left as well as the same for my right foot. But Kuŋśi has different flowers on the sides of her left and right foot. The symmetry in her case comes from the same design in toto (green) on left and right feet.

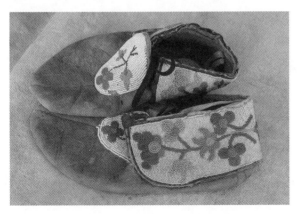

Sagadaśiŋ's (Sarah Renville LaBatte's) soft-sole moccasins.

My dad said haŋpikceka (ordinary moccasins) were unbeaded moccasins, whilst haŋpa śipto was the beaded moccasins. I just use the word haŋpa.

I don't believe there is a checklist for identifying a certain moccasin as belonging to a certain tribe. There can be too many variables. You have to know the maker's name and which tribe the artist was from. When I look at my moccasins, I can name certain things which I incorporate in my moccasins, but there are exceptions. I changed up a few things from the pattern of the Isaŋati moccasins; they are not quite like Kuŋśi's. And I have already seen the varieties of Isaŋati floral. Some just bead the flower on buckskin without background, and it may appear that some are beaded on black cloth like the Ḣaḣatoŋwaŋ (Ojibwe).

I don't think anyone could afford to buy these Isaŋati center-seam moccasins, since it takes forever to bead the background. Kuŋśi must

Dakota treaty delegation to Washington, DC, 1858. Standing: Joseph R. Brown, Antoine Joseph (Joe) Campbell, Caŋḣpi Yuha (Has a War Club), Andrew Robertson, Hiŋhaŋ Duta (Red Owl), Thomas A. Robertson, Nathaniel R. Brown. Seated: Maŋkato, Wapahaśa III, Henry Belland. Wapahaśa wears Isaŋati-style moccasins. Photograph by Charles DeForest Fredericks, Minnesota Historical Society collections have had a lot of patience, or else she must have been a lot faster than me. I can see why some Isaŋati beadwork has no background, just the beaded flower on beautiful brain-tanned buckskin.

When I sewed in the tongue, I could see the similarities with the Ḣaḣatoŋwaŋ, with the Hotaŋke (Ho-Chunk), and with other woodland tribes. They all have the basic one-piece leather, both for the sole and the vamp; they just have their peculiarities.

There's a picture of the Mdewakaŋtoŋwaŋ chiefs in Washington in 1858, showing Wapaḣaṡa sitting in front with the other chiefs standing behind. Wapaḣaṡa has on a pair of mocs like this.

• • • •

I beaded my first vest nearly thirty years ago. When I started the vest, my plan was to just bead the front panels red, with a design on the back. However, as I was beading, I was having second thoughts and thought a design should be on the front. But I had no idea what to put there, and I was getting close to where I needed to start a design—

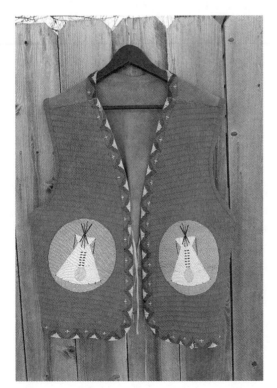

Dekṡi Super's beaded vest.

almost panicking. I went to bed that night, and I saw this tipi design in my dreams. I was in that state of sleep/awake because I was aware that I should get up to draw it out lest I forget it. But I was too sleepy, so didn't. And when I woke up that morning, I had no memory of that until the afternoon when I started beading again and I remembered. So that was where that design came from. Some years later, my aunt was showing some of my grandfather's writings when the name of Hotoŋtoŋna's first wife came up, Tipiojaŋjaŋwiŋ. Tipiojaŋjaŋwiŋ means "Lighted Tipi Woman" and that was the design I put on that first vest. Man, that name just about knocked me over, since I recognized that as my design.

· · · ·

Art is a subjective endeavor in that what I like, maybe someone else doesn't like, and vice versa. But with that said, in order for me to be satisfied with the art I produce, I must become proficient in both the craft part and the artistic part—neither one is more important than the other. As far as the craft part goes, I had to learn to use certain materials (buckskin) and stringing material (sinew) and to be proficient in their use. And then, of course, I had to have an artistic eye for color and design. It can be seen that deficiencies in either will produce art which would not be satisfactory. I could have the best artistic capabilities, but if I did not execute properly, it would not look good to most people. On the other hand, if I was excellent in the craft part but had no artistic eye, it would also be deficient in my eyes.

· · · ·

I got started with beading over thirty years ago. I had made a big change in my life—I sobered up. I noticed other Indian people that had sobered up and became "Super Indian." I had thought, I'm just satisfied I'm sober. Maybe a year in, I noticed I was missing something. There was a spiritual aspect of my being that was missing. I looked into my Dakota ways and decided to dance. Dance regalia cost a lot of money, so I decided I would make my own. Surprisingly, my first beadwork turned out pretty good, and I was satisfied with it.

When I started to make my regalia, I picked up leather from Tandy and beaded on that. I remember a guy came up to me at a powwow and said, "I like your beadwork. You did a good job with that." I said, "Yeah, but look at my fingers"—my fingers were beat up and full of Band-Aids. He said, "Oh, you got to use Indian-tan buck skin; that's just like cloth." "Where do you get that?" And that's when Dad told me how. Through his explanations and help, I got started.

• • • •

It's really just a big circle I am treading on. I am on that part of the circle where I am trimming out the moccasin again as I have finished up the beading. I think I can do this in my sleep. I remember when Kuŋśi Elizabeth was in a coma and the community members were made aware of this, so we all went to the hospital to say our goodbyes.

Deksi Super beading.

Though she was in a coma, she was moving her hands as if she were sewing. I suppose that was such a habit for her, and perhaps my last days will be such. There is a Dakota story of a kuŋśi who is constantly making something and never gets done because her śuŋka unravels her work when she is not attending to the job, and thus the world will end whenever she gets done. I think the job she was doing was edging beadwork—my least favorite chore in making moccasins as it is so tedious, making progress of a quarter inch per stitch. When I am edging around the tongue, it seems it will never end.

When I have the moccasin soles cut out, I sew them onto the sides. I put the smooth side, the former hair side, on the inside, because that is the stronger side of the hide and there is much tension when sewing it on. The hide is about a quarter inch thick. Others do the reverse. Before I sew on, I rub mink oil on the sole bottoms and the edges. After a while, moccasins become flat pancake moccasins. I never liked that look. I want the sides to always stand up as if they are new. So, I came up with the idea of taking deer rawhide covered with trade cloth and sewing it on the sides, so the stiffness keeps the sides up. Then, of course, sew bias tape around the edges. Deer rawhide

The finished moccasins.

is thin enough so that it does not hamper turning the moccasin, yet thick enough to keep the side up.

• • • •

The goal in sewing the moccasin onto the sole is to get it on right. I make two marks on the moccasin and on the sole, and if I line them up, this ensures that the tongue will be straight across. To accomplish this, it is necessary to start at the middle of the sole in back. When I sew the moccasin top to the sole, I sew halfway through the thickness of the sole. When the sole is not very thick, as in the case of rawhide, I use an old Indian trick: I rub the thickness of the sole with a butter knife or the edge of a letter opener, and that thickens up the edge of the sole so it is much easier to sew through the thickness. There— now I have given up all my secrets.

• • • •

When I taught a haŋpa-making class here, I focused on technique rather than artistic expression. With that in mind, all five of my students used one of my moccasin designs, and they picked the colors. When they were done, all five pairs of moccasins looked unique, and it would take a concerted effort to notice that they all had the same design. So that's the lesson here: that with color variations and small changes to the design, a whole new moccasin is possible.

Once a group of my apprentices displayed their work at Jackpot Junction Casino. They showed their first moccasins, smoked deer hide, and their wahiŋkte. We had fine food and also had a silent-auction fundraiser. I donated a hand drum. Kudos to the apprentices; they made the classes enjoyable, and I'm glad to have passed on the brain-tan knowledge. I always get choked up when I tell about Dad teaching me, because it almost did not happen. I was so sure he knew nothing about making buckskin. In my early days of making moccasins, I brought back a pair to show him. Dad, usually pretty stoic, got kind of emotional and said he thought this was a lost art, just a part of history. He kept holding the moccasins and rubbing the beadwork. I couldn't help but to give them to him then. Oh, he was so happy. Dad was born in 1900 and died in 1996, one month short of his ninety-sixth birthday.

Drum Making

Back in the '50s my parents made small drums from gallon tin cans: they glued some paper around the can and cut rubber heads out of old inner tubes. They sold them to some company in St. Paul. We had them stacked in the house, and occasionally it would get too hot and a drumhead would pop. We loaded them up into our car to deliver them to St. Paul. I can't imagine my parents making much money off this adventure, but maybe that's how I got my idea and skills for making "real authentic Dakota drums."

• • • •

Years ago, I entered a powwow drum I made in an art show. I took the drum to the show the day before and told the officials about how I make them, using thirty boards, beveled at six degrees. The next day, one of the officials questioned me about the thirty boards. He was sure I bent plywood around, because he said he could not find a joint in the whole drum, so it had to be bent. One of the greatest compliments ever. That's my job—to make the joints not visible.

• • • •

When you cut lace for a powwow drum, cut what you think should be enough, then double it, and that should be enough. That sage is applicable when lacing hand drums, too. I don't think I ever cut too much lace on the first go-around.

• • • •

I have been thinking about painting my hand drums with Dakota foods and medicines, such as tewapa (root of the white lily), siŋk-petawote (sweet flag), wamnaheza (Indian corn), caŋȟdohu apema-daska (plantain), etc. What will be missing is pejuhutazizi, as there is no consensus what it is. I have my opinion but am not sure. When I was a teenager, I asked an elder here at Pejuhutazizi about the yellow medicine and what it was for. He answered kind of embarrassingly by pointing to his crotch and said it was for that. Sensing his being uncomfortable, I never pursued it further by asking to show me the plant and its uses.

• • • •

There is no consensus today on exactly which plant is pejuhutazizi, yellow medicine. Some believe it is the root of the moonseed plant; others say the root of gentian. Another option is ginseng. The *Granite Falls Tribune* reported on June 28, 1887, that "Fourteen Indians camped near town Thursday. They came from Redwood and are pulling ginseng near Hawk Creek." A *Minneapolis Star Tribune* article about the Upper Sioux Indian Reservation, published September 2, 1978, notes that "The Dakota call their reservation Pejuhutazizi Village after the ginseng root that their ancestors dug up to cure fevers and colds. The county in which they live, Yellow Medicine County, is also named for ginseng." In 2019, the Minnesota Arboretum showcased indigenous plants of Minnesota, including ginseng. The root is yellow and can sometimes resemble a human form, just like the moonseed root. Ginseng is considered beneficial for men's sexual health, which may explain the response of the male elder when Dekṡi asked about pejuhutazizi.

Among the Dakota, when decisions had to be made that affected the band or tribe, the chief and head-men called for the erection of a Tiyotipi, a Soldiers' Lodge, in the center of the camp circle. A woman who was considered the best tipi maker was asked to provide the tipi for this purpose. The buffalo hunt, war, or when and where to move to winter camp were typical topics. After the decision(s), which had to be unanimous (to eliminate halfhearted efforts or sabotage), the eyapaha or camp crier announced the decisions

Three of Dekṡi Super's drums.

to the camp at large. We made camp in the shape of the horns of the buffalo, so I decided maybe that would be a good picture to paint on my drums. There are two other Dakota names for tribes describing their camp circle: The Omaha were given the name of Oyate Noŋpa (Two Nations) in recognition that they camped in two concentric circles. The Ponca were given the name of Oyate Yamni (Three Nations) because they camped in three concentric circles. Ho, hecetu, mitakuye owasiŋ.

Wacipi

Dad and his mother were powwow people in the early 1900s. Dad told me he and his mother drove a team and wagon to Fort Thompson for powwow and camped on the James River. Can you imagine driving there with a team and no roads? It was all cross-country, according to Dad. They even went to Ḣaḣatoŋwaŋ country for powwow. Dad was born in 1900, so this took place in the early 1900s, when he was a child, probably five or six years old. They went to the White Earth powwow, and there they had a giveaway and somebody gave Dad a trained dog and wagon. Because the dog was trained in Chippewa, the man who gave him the dog taught him the commands in Chippewa, such as gee, haw, and whoa, I suspect. What a great gift for a young child, as Dad said he enjoyed that immensely. I have heard other relatives, besides Dad, tell of this event.

• • • •

The White Earth Reservation, one of seven Ojibwe reservations in Minnesota, has held an annual powwow since 1873. At that time, government agents were actively suppressing Native ceremonies, but they permitted the band to hold this event "to celebrate their removal from Gull Lake to White Earth," as anthropologist Frances Densmore put it.

I remember when Old Agency, Sisseton, had a powwow on Labor Day weekend. That was almost as big as the Fourth of July powwow. Oh, man, I had fun there. It was also kind of sad, because that was the end of the powwow season and time to go back to school. I don't remember indoor powwows in those days.

Back in the early '60s at the Sisseton powwow, you could have nothing wašicuŋ on your outfit. No sunglasses or any type of glasses, no watches. Anything that would take away from what an "authentic" Dakota would wear, I guess. You were disqualified if you broke those rules. The eyapaha, perhaps Burton Stepp, would occasionally remind the dancers of this rule. I don't know if they checked under the cehnake (breechcloth), to see if they were wearing what the Scotsman has on under his kilt—namely, nothing.

The contest was also run differently. On the first go-around, a number of dancers were picked, and subsequently other dancers were picked in the following sessions. Then, Sunday, those dancers would dance off for the places. In other words, there was no point system, as they have today. So if you were not picked on Friday night, you could just quit dancing. The Men's Fancy was the biggest, most popular dance group. The Men's Traditional was pretty skimpy, with no fancy beadwork—a pretty plain-Jane dance.

• • • •

It isn't unusual to see Germans at summer powwows. I can spot them by their German-accented English, or merely their speaking German. On several occasions, I have come up to them in my dance regalia and in German asked if they come from Germany. At first there is this stunned second or so of silence, and I can see that their eyes and their ears are in conflict. There is no recognition of what is happening. So, I continue in German, saying, "Oh, it only appears that I am Indian, but I am really German." Another stunned silence of disbelief. And then, after a while, a smile and the truth comes to them: "Ah, you are an Indian who speaks German." Next time this happens, though, I want to turn the table and ask them, "Bitte, darf ich dein bild machen?"—"Please, can I take your picture?"

I don't use wase (war paint) because I don't want to mess up my pretty looks. No, I tried once and sweat messed it up and it ran. Then I kept scratching my face, as it itched, and by the time the session was over, the paint looked terrible. And if it covered my face totally, I might scare myself if I walked by a mirror.

• • • •

Do you still get shivers down your back when you come in Grand Entry with a beautiful song—where you are not conscious of your feet, where the drum seems to be dancing for you, or you're under its control, being totally in sync with the drum? Where that good feeling just overtakes your body? I am remembering a song from perhaps twenty years ago by a Canadian drum— "Dakota Hotaiŋ," or "Elk's Whistle"—that had words like this: "Oiyukipiyaŋ waci wau . . ." I come in dancing beautifully. Man, that was and is a beautiful song from yesteryear. I always look forward to that first outdoor powwow; I very seldom dance indoors. That's not a judgment, just my choice. I understand some make their living that way.

When I no longer have fun dancing, that's when I'll quit.

Dakota Presbytery

When I was growing up, the church played a central part in the community, and I believe it had reached its heyday in my youth—but, of course, those older than me may think it was earlier. Over the years, that has changed by church membership dropping. But at that earlier time, the church was full, with beautiful Dakota odowaŋpi being sung "to the rafters." Nowadays, very few are proficient in our hymns, and we are losing those elders who experienced this beautiful time. In 2016, we lost one of our elders, Tahaŋśi Dean Blue. He followed in his parents' footsteps by being a pillar in our church and community, and he is greatly missed in both arenas.

I suppose it was mandatory to go to church when I was a kid, though it never felt like a burden; more as a fellowship of others who "had" to go to church also. But from this perspective, it feels more like a cultural experience—the services were conducted in Dakota—

Dekši Super dancing.

than a religious indoctrination. Grandpa Waŋbdiska didn't come to church every Sunday, though he lived next door to the church. As a kid, I mentioned that to Mom, that Grandpa doesn't have to come to church every Sunday. I just figured that was the benefit of being an elder. Years later, I was in church with Mom when we sang an English hymn—a rare event, and it always seemed to be "What a Friend We Have in Jesus," the only English song we knew, I suspect. I didn't sing, and Mom quickly mentioned, "Oh, you're just like your grandpa, who also wouldn't sing English, only Dakota odowaŋ."

• • • •

Conkicaŋkse means Where They Cut or Gather Wood, as I understand it from the elders of my youth. This name refers to Fort Thompson and the Presbyterian Church there. In my youth, our Dakota Presbyterian churches were all called by their Dakota names and mostly all do yet today. At Sisseton there is the Presbyterian church near Old Agency Village called Goodwill Presbyterian or, in Dakota, Tawaciŋ Waśte, meaning good will, good mind, or good disposition. Other Dakota place names come to mind: Maka Saŋ, Maya Saŋ, Bde Caŋ, of course Pejuhutazizi, Iyakaptapi, and others in Montana which I can't remember. I wonder how long before these names will be forgotten and only a memory.

• • • •

When I was a youngster, for some reason, I had a difficult time pronouncing this Dakota word, Okodakiciye. That word was used in reference to one of our Presbyterian meetings. The Congregationalists and the Presbyterians had a joint meeting called the Okodakiciye, and in English it was called the Mission Meeting. One year it was hosted by a Congregationalist church, and the next meeting was hosted by a Dakota Presbyterian church. One can see the root word of koda, or kola in the Lakota version, so it meant an association meeting of common interest or so. Now I see it being used for veteran organizations. It is good to hear that word again.

• • • •

My mom, Joyce, with her younger siblings Julie and Super. They were attending an Okodakiciye at Goodwill Presbyterian Church on the Sisseton Reservation in the late 1950s.

I knew I was getting old when I saw a picture of the Dakota Presbyterian ministers from the '50s and I could name eight or nine of the ministers, and I thought I will just go ask—ask who? Who is older than me and could name the rest? I could not think of anyone. I recognize Floyd Heminger, Guy Rondell, Steve Spider, Howard Orcutt, Sid Byrd, Doctor Phillips, Hunter Keen, Enoch LaPointe, and I think Cecil Corbett. The other five I don't know. Paul Fire Cloud was not in here, so it had to be from the '50s, as Paul was not ordained until '61 or '62. Paul was ordained jointly by the then Mankato Presbytery and Dakota Presbytery.

• • • •

We have such beautiful hymns in our *Dakota Odowaŋ.* I guess I must have been in elementary school when I learned the Dakota numbers—the big numbers—by figuring out the logic involved when the minister in church announced the Dakota odowaŋ we were to sing. I would open up my hymnal to that song and ask my mother if that were the song. She would nod yes. So, soon I will sing, and Karen, my partner, will play Dakota Odowaŋ wikcemna yamni sam num (ten threes and two more, i.e., thirty-two). My dad taught me Dakota Odowaŋ #32. We Presbyterians have very slow, staid, mournful songs—I am not sure of the correct word, but certainly no fast gospel songs. Yet this Dakota Odowaŋ #32 is somewhat of an exception, as it is kind of fast with almost a march beat. We Presbyterians also have little ritual compared to others. So, it was somewhat of a surprise for me that at the funeral of Rev. Herbert Crawford at the Flandreau First Presbyterian Church, the Dakota Presbyterian ministers brought in his casket at the beginning of the funeral with this hymn. The congregation all stood and sang this song. What a moving thing to witness. It sends shivers up my spine even today, thinking about that.

• • • •

Oh, how I remember Christmas as a child. During the Christmas service, Norman Blue would walk up to the minister to whisper something in his ear or hand him a note. The minister would announce that Waziya had just left the North Pole! There would be progress reports throughout the service, bringing updates on his travels. Santa was visiting the Fort Peck Reservation churches and was headed south. Oh, we children would get all excited that Santa would be here soon. And just as the sermon was done, Santa would enter. Of course, Waziya couldn't talk, so he used Norman as his mouthpiece. I remember asking Mom if I could go outside to see the reindeer, but no—oh, how disappointed I was. Waziya said he could not stay long since he was afraid the Ross boys (meaning Lanny and Pete, both good hunters) might shoot his reindeer. Such were the banters of Waziya as told through Norman. Oh, all you young people who rail against colonization and Christianity, you missed a lot of fun and excitement.

My tahaŋśi was sitting in jail for thirty days over Christmas for a DWI, but the sheriff let him out to attend our Christmas service. So, he and Deputy Brandt show up at church—thank God no handcuffs. I guess the opportunity to spend some time out overrode any embarrassment. I don't think this kind of thing happens anymore. This was the late '50s or early '60s, so we were much like *Mayberry RFD* back then. I am sure Tahaŋśi was the talk of the reservation.

Karen goes to the church every year to help bag candy for the Christmas service. Oh man, that tradition goes back all my life and probably way before. Dad told us about his Christmas services at St. Mary's. He said they also went to other churches' services, too. He talked about getting and distributing whole barrels of apples. Dad was raised Episcopal but became a Presbyterian when he married Mom. I wonder if waśicuŋ congregations give out candy like we do.

After our Christmas service, we have a meal, and Karen and I bring paśdayapi. Karen cuts up the vegetables and I do the meat.

In my youth, we always had our Christmas service on the 24th or 25th, depending on the Flandreau First Presbyterian Church, as we shared a minister with them. The ministers I can remember include Steve Spider, Howard Orcutt, Floyd Heminger, and Paul Fire Cloud. With the exception of Orcutt, all of them held services in Dakota. A funny thing about our *Dakota Odowaŋ* hymnal is that there are no Christmas songs in there—so we never sang Christmas songs. A tradition maybe from the early missionaries, as that was the status quo in the 1800s, when Christmas was not a big celebration as it is today. One Christmas that stands out in my memory is the year our car's headlights went on the blink, and we had no lights, so I thought we wouldn't make it to church. We were all loaded in the car with presents and people. Dad just got a flashlight and Gordy held it out the window, and we made it to church. Anybody remember when we took all the presents to church and after Santa came, they were all handed out and we had to bring them all home again? Maybe that was the tradition only in our church.

Our Dakota Hymn #141, "Lac qui Parle," the hymn reported to have been sung at the hanging of the thirty-eight, has really gained some popularity in the last few years. This song is in our *Dakota Odowaŋ* Presbyterian hymnal. In my youth, we rarely, if ever, sang

Dakota Odowaŋ #141, Lac qui Parle. Smithsonian Institution

this song at Pejuhutazizi Presbyterian. I don't know about the other Dakota churches, but we have been singing this at our Christmas service these past years. A great deal of emotion emanates from this song, from the story attached to it, I suspect. This song has been translated and put into the mainstream Presbyterian hymnals.

• • • •

When I was in high school and maybe in college, I suffered from cluster headaches. They are much more painful than migraines, and as the name says, they come in clusters. I had mine two to three times per day for about a month, and then they went away for three months, then returned. It was almost like clockwork: as the three months came closer, I seemed to expect them. One time I had an especially painful one, and I retreated to the basement where it was dark and quiet, as light and noise aggravated my head. My thoughts were only on how to stop this pain, and I thought of shooting myself to get it over with. Fortunately, we had only long guns, no handguns, and I didn't think I could accomplish Selbstmord with that. That day, Mom hosted the Ladies' Aid at our house, and they started to sing Dakota Odowaŋ #27. It translates as "God is everywhere, He is in Heaven, He is on earth, He watches over me." From that song, the pain slowly retreated, and I was okay—no more thoughts of suicide. I always think that song saved my life in some ways. After some years, the cluster headaches left and never came back. So, whether it is physical or mental torment, it is still pure hell and can result in Selbstmord.

• • • •

Sundays in my youth always seemed happy and joyous. After supper, we went back to church for the evening service. There never seemed to be as many as the 11:00 AM service. We always seemed to sing Dakota Odowaŋ #111, which I later came to call the evening song: "Htayetu aomahaŋzi, taku waŋ awacaŋmi . . ." It must have been after I went to college that the evening service was dropped. Now, attendance is sparse even at our morning service. I just hope Pejuhutazizi Church holds out at least as long as I am alive. I was baptized there, married there, and I hope I go out there. Yes, things change.

Funerals

Back in my youth, it was standard practice for the men in our community to dig the grave of one of our own. And so was the case in this story, which took place back in the early 1960s. I believe I am the only one left alive who witnessed this event. Fortunately, both of my brothers were back from the service, and I felt kind of proud to walk up to Doncaster Cemetery with them to help dig the grave. Someone from the cemetery had marked out the grave, and so we all took turns digging. Halfway done, we started to notice rotten wood, and sure enough we hit a grave. So, we moved over and proceeded to dig again. One of our elders was down in the hole digging, and suddenly the side wall caved in and exposed another grave. He jumped out of there and ran away scared. We all had our chance to jump back in and look. The ground did not cave in from the top but left a cavity where the bones were clearly visible. Eerie, yes.

• • • •

I am reminded of a story or experience Dad told me long time ago. He happened to be hunting on Sisseton Reservation, where he was raised. He was hunting in a patch of woods in the winter—cold and windy. This had to be in the 1910s, as he said he was just a youngster. He started to hear a noise but paid no attention because the wind was blowing so hard. It was a screeching noise and constant. He happened to look up into the trees and saw this skeleton blowing in the wind. He said at one time we Dakota buried our dead in trees, and after a year the family took the bones down and buried them. Dad intimated that this one was calling to get his attention, showing that he was still up in the trees.

• • • •

In Dad's time, it was the practice to have the wake and funeral in the deceased's home, and of course, no one at that time was embalmed. It was winter when they had the wake for this person, and they had the coffin set up in the house. It became warm in the house, with the woodstove and with all the people in attendance. The deceased suddenly sat up; they cleared the house in seconds, Dad said. Cooler heads prevailed, and they surmised that because of the heat his muscles tightened and thus he sat up. They returned him to the supine position, and the services continued. But if I was there, I would have been the first one out—even if I had to climb over people.

• • • •

This grandpa died, and he would occasionally show up in familiar surroundings, sitting in his favorite chair. He made himself visible to his grandkids, and they became scared. "Ha! We saw Grandpa sitting over there!" This upset his widow, and she matter-of-factly went in where he made himself known and scolded him for scaring the grandkids. I guess this was enough, because he never showed up again. I knew these people. When I heard this, I was astounded because she was not scared but just accepted this as quite normal.

• • • •

When I was building my house, I came down from St. Paul, where I lived then, and stayed at my parents' home while I built. Of course, I had to bring along my springer spaniel, as he went everywhere I went. After being there for a while, Gus started to accept my parents' home as his and became protective. My brother came home from Fort Yates late one night and he just came in, but Gus thought he was an intruder and stopped him by barking and growling at him. Finally, Wayne kicked him and made Gus even more mad. I rescued the situation, but from that time on, Gus hated Wayne and growled at him every time he saw him. Perhaps a year or so later, Wayne died, and my mother asked me to speak at his wake addressing his alcoholism, as Mom did not want to sweep the cause of his death under the rug, so to speak. So I spoke and then went to bed in my uncompleted house across the road from the community center. Late at night, Gus got up and went to the door, growling and barking. I turned on the light, and he was slowly backing up but continuing to bark and growl, just as he did when he encountered Wayne previously. I soon recognized that Wayne was paying a visit, as I thought he might have liked what I said earlier at the wake. I have no doubt that that was my brother, even though he was visible only to Gus. That is my ghost story, but I was not even scared and in fact addressed him by name.

• • • •

This story is kind of along the lines of the story of the wife attending her husband's funeral, when she asked her son to check the casket to make sure that the man the eulogist was talking about was his father, since she did not recognize him as her husband. One year at our powwow, there was a special dance for recognition or honoring a member here. The eyapaha was talking about him when this man from a neighboring reservation came to my mom to ask who they were talking about, because similarly, he did not recognize him. Mom, in her most unjudgmental fashion, merely said, "Oh, he was a funny man." I understand the speaker for the family may have been interested in a good remuneration, so that's why he said what he said. I wonder if there is anyone who is concerned about the lies which may be told at his/her funeral or rite. Years ago, when I was a practicing alcoholic, I came upon an article in *Psychology Today* about introspection—looking inside to take an accounting of one's life, to see if one were satisfied. In AA parlance, taking one's inventory. This was the first step, I suppose, for me to consider sobering up. But more than sobering up—making and living a respectable life.

• • • •

It must have been close to forty years ago that I was telling Curt Williams about my grandmother's last day in the hospital. Grandma told Mom and me that there were these people—who she named— who came to visit her, but they didn't speak. She said she talked to them in Ojibwe first, then Dakota, and then English, but they did not respond. After we left, I asked Mom about that, and she said, "Oh my gosh, those people have been dead fifty years." Later that night, Grandma died. Only in retrospect do I understand that those people were there to help her across. After I told Curt this, he told me his story about his mother, Haugie Williams. It seems she had been in the hospital a number of days, and she seemed to be quite ill and ailing. Curt said that evening when he came to see her, she told him that she was going home. Of course, he took her statement literally and knew she wasn't fit to go home. She died that night. It seems to me those old Indian people knew a lot about death and were not scared of it but seemed to accept. I hope to learn from my elders.

• • • •

I remember years ago after I sobered up and got into my artwork— beading, making buckskin, and making drums—Mom said, "Oh, your grandpa Waŋbdiska would be so proud of you." So maybe it is still good to make your ancestors proud of you—they still know. Your descendants won't appreciate you until you're gone, so don't worry about that, as that is normal.

Grandpa Waŋbdiska has been gone since 1958, but he is still remembered fondly by those who knew him. Since we are but a minuscule aspect in the spectrum of time, I suppose we want to also be remembered sixty-some years later. But not so much as to be famous but to be known as a decent human being, which Waŋbdiska certainly was. When Grandfather Waŋbdiska died, I knew he had some stature and renown because the ministers from Sisseton came to his funeral. Our minister was Rev. Steve Spider, but Rev. Abe Crawford did the funeral service. That is quite an honor when you recognize that Grandpa was a wašicuŋ, but thoroughly a Dakota in speech and manner. In fact, I thought he was Dakota when I was young, as he rarely spoke English; at the time, nearly everybody spoke Dakota.

Mother often talked glowingly of her dad and loved and respected him much. That goes for everyone in our family and extended family, even though he was kind of a gruff character, if I may so describe without disrespect. He never minced his words and told you the truth—to do otherwise was to enable bad behavior and do more harm. My siblings have also said I am like that—"Oh, you're just like Grandpa." I have heard that more than once. Anyway, for the above reason, I was astounded when Mother talked late in life about going to the spirit world, and the first one she was looking for was Dad. I told her he would be there waiting for her. They were married well over sixty years—I don't know the exact number. But what a tribute to Dad and their marriage and relationship.

• • • •

When we all reach the spirit world and greet all those that played a part in our life, we will greet them with gratitude and a hug, for each of them brought gifts to us in our lives. Especially those who we might have called our tormentors, for they gave us the opportunity to rise above pettiness, anger, and hate and instead show love and forgiveness. We will then fully understand the grand illusion of life and maybe learn to "wear life lightly as a loose garment." And also fully understand Shakespeare's observation that "all the world's a stage," and we make our entrances and our exits.

Stories Deliver Heroes

The admiration of family and community heroes, the honor of ancestry, and the dedication to one's people are all gained through story. Through story, heroes are kept alive in the minds of the people.

Nasuna Taŋka

In 1862 and 1863, all the Sioux Indians, except for a few families, were driven out of Minnesota. They were the Sisitoŋwaŋ, Waȟpetoŋwaŋ, Mdewakaŋtoŋwaŋ, and Waȟpekute, the latter two bands being called Santee.

For the next few years, they ranged along the Missouri River near Bismarck and up into North Dakota and Montana. There was good buffalo hunting along the river, although sometimes they had to go farther west to find the best herds. Of course, they were associated with and had close contact with the western people, and they often had their villages and communities side by side.

One summer, rather late in the season, when they were camped along the river, they noticed smoke far up the stream. As they knew no village was located in that direction, they wondered what the smoke was or could be. After watching it for some time, they could see that it was moving. They couldn't understand what it was, but of course, naturally, they kept watching it.

As it kept moving, they could see that it was gradually coming nearer, but as yet, nothing could be seen. After some time, however, the source of the smoke came into view. It was a steamboat on the Missouri River, which had gone up the stream in the early summer and was now coming back downstream with the current.

The Indians stood on the shore and the hills and bluffs along the river, watching the boat. It was quite a sight to them, as none had ever seen such a large boat before. Compared to their canoes, it was an enormous affair that had quite a number of people on it and was so large that those people could walk around on it easily, rather than having to sit still in the bottom as in a canoe, for fear of tipping it over.

In this story, Grandpa Fred is discussing the Dakota who fled Minnesota at the end of the war.

Because steamboats had been traveling the Mississippi and Minnesota Rivers since the 1820s, it is likely that these Dakota has already seen one. Grandpa Fred's account matches in many details stories told by white historians of a mackinaw boat carrying twenty-seven miners, a woman, and two children who were returning from the Idaho gold fields with a large amount of gold dust in August 1863. The white historians describe the Dakota savagely attacking the boat without provocation and killing all its passengers.

But Red Blanket, a woman of Shakopee's band who was an eyewitness to the events, left a story that supports Grandpa Fred's version. Journalist Joseph Henry Taylor of Yankton, South Dakota, visited the Santee Reservation in 1868 and interviewed her. In August 1863, she was in a large camp of "Santee," Sisitoŋwaŋ, and Ihaŋktoŋwaŋna that had been evading Sibley's soldiers. They were hunting buffalo, camped in a deep coulee on the Missouri. The incident began when a passing mackinaw boat came upon an elderly Dakota man who was fishing near a sandbar (a place Taylor identified as Burnt Creek Bar, just north of what is now Bismarck) while Red Blanket and other women were washing clothes. When the elder realized the boat was drifting near the sandbar, she said, "He arose and made the blanket signal to keep out in the main stream. Next came a puff of smoke and a rifle report from the boat and the old man fell over. Then we all screamed and ran until we met our husbands and brothers with their guns, bows and arrows." In the following battle, "several of our fighters procured logs and rolled across the bar, firing from behind." The attackers killed all who were on the boat; Red Blanket reported nearly thirty deaths among the Dakota. She also described their finding "belts of what we thought was wet or bad powder." In 1876, Taylor interviewed Whistling Bear, an Arikara man, whose account of the gold on this boat parallels Grandpa Fred's. Taylor chose not to publish these accounts until 1897, in a book of reminiscences. Subsequent retellings in other publications by white historians delete the information about who fired first; Clement Augustus Lounsberry ends his account, "For some unexplained reason, certain individuals who were believed to have had some knowledge of it refused to disclose anything."

In the white man's rumors of this steamboat episode, they are supposed to have been attacked by hostile Indians, but this is not true. The Indians acted peaceably toward the boat and made no demonstration against it until they were compelled to do so in self-defense. The crew of the steamboat were the hostiles.

When they saw so many Indians along the shore, they got very arrogant. They had some kind of a small cannon on the boat. This they loaded and discharged at the Indians along the shore, although it did no harm. Some thought no bullets or balls were used but that it was discharged for the noise.

One certain person who wore a red coat or jacket was the one who operated the gun. When he came on deck, the Indians would all run for cover, and then after the report of the gun, they would all come out of hiding and stand on the shore watching the strange fire boat again. This happened many times, but no demonstrations against the boat were made, despite the haughty acts of the boat crew.

A crier was sent out among the people, ordering them to make no hostile acts toward the boat, as they didn't want trouble with the white people. They mentioned the traders' outbreak in Minnesota in 1862 and said they did not want to get involved in anything like that again.

Late in the summer, the water gets low in the Missouri and there are numerous sandbars, some in the middle of the river and others projecting out from the shore toward the middle of the stream. The boat was now near a sandbar that ran out into the stream from the shore, and it would pass very close to the point of the bar.

Among the western people was an old man who was a retired chief, named Nasuna Taŋka. With all the good intentions, he wished to avoid any trouble and decided to do what he could to show that they had no hostile intentions toward the boat or the crew. So, he dressed himself in his best buckskin clothing and took a pipestone peace pipe with him and went out onto the point of the bar where the boat would pass very close.

He stood on the point of the bar, presenting the peace pipe as the boat passed. For no reason at all and knowing that the old man was not armed, one of the crew on the boat took up a gun and shot and killed him when they knew he was on a peaceful mission. That was too much uncalled-for hostility for the people to stand. Although the council had

This Nasuna Taŋka may have been the father of Pahtaŋka or Nasula Taŋka (Big Head or Big Brain), an Ihaŋktoŋwaŋna leader (1838–1889) who shared his father's name (but used a Lakota spelling). If so, the retired chief survived this attack, because he was captured after the Massacre of Whitestone Hill, September 3–5, 1863. General Alfred Sully's troops attacked a peaceful hunting camp of Ihaŋktoŋwaŋna, Lakota, and Dakota. They took Nasuna Taŋka and other captives to Crow Creek, where he died. The son was a signer of the Treaty of Fort Laramie of 1868 and became a leader at the Standing Rock Reservation.

ordered that no demonstration was to be made against the boat and had ordered a crier to spread the decree among the people, this was now overlooked.

The old man that was killed had been a chief but on account of his age had retired and let younger men take his place. He was much beloved and honored by his people. He was also known among the Waḣpetoŋwaŋ people of western Minnesota. Once long before, he had spent a winter in the Yellow Medicine vicinity that is now Granite Falls, Minnesota.

So, the people saw that there was no making peace with the steamboat crew. Regardless of what the council had decreed earlier, they now said, "Now we will go for them. Now we will fight them and give them what they want." Then everyone took up arms and began shooting at the boat. Whenever anyone appeared on the boat, he was met by a volley of shots. Some used guns and some bows and arrows.

A big log of driftwood was rolled into the water, and some warriors swam in its shelter and maneuvered it toward the boat. When they had a chance, one would rise up now and then and take a shot at the crew on the boat as one might appear.

After this attack had gone on for some time, a lucky shot either killed or seriously wounded the steersman. No one else on the boat seemed to be able to steer it, or possibly no one dared to come out of the shelter of the cabin and they were trusting to luck that the boat would follow the deep water of the stream safely. It drifted with the current for a while, swinging crazily from one side of the stream to the other, just as the current happened to take it.

As the water was low, there were many shallow places, and finally it struck a sandbar and came to a stop. Nothing could be done now. The boat was there to stay.

Everyone now with arms attacked the boat and made short work of those that were left of the crew. Next, they ransacked the boat and took everything useful they could find. It was generally believed that this boat had been up in Montana, where they had found gold, and that they had been washing gold up there all summer.

Among the cargo of the boat was a large pile of small canvas or buckskin sacks filled with gold dust, but the Indians didn't realize what it was, but they did think it was something that the white people valued highly. As they had no use for it and it was only a lure to bring other intruders, they threw all the sacks of gold dust into the river. But one man took two of the sacks with him. Another took a handful of the dust and tied it up in a piece of buckskin and put it in his bullet pouch.

Among the Indians was a mixed-blood trader who had a small stock of goods such as the Indians might need. His name was Pejiskuya (Sweet Medicine) from the Yellow Medicine vicinity. This trader got hold of these two sacks and probably gave only a very small fraction of their real value, but probably he had no idea of what the stuff was and only traded for it on a gamble.

Later, this trader sold these two sacks to a regular large trader from Canada who seemed to have a pretty good idea of its value. He gave him a good horse and saddle and a supply of other goods. He also wrote a paper as a receipt, and attached was a letter to his company telling of the deal and instructing his company to investigate, and if he had not paid a fair price, they were to pay him some more and make a reasonable payment for the gold. No one ever heard what became of the handful that was stored away in a bullet pouch.

The trader, Pejiskuya, kept the papers he had received from the Canadian company and expected sometime to be able to go to Canada with his document and hunt up the headquarters of the company, but he never was able to make the trip. Maybe some of his descendants kept the paper, but not knowing what it was, it probably was destroyed.

Many Feathers/Ornaments

A story is told of how long ago, a large Mandan war party came from the Missouri River, where their homes were, to make a raid on any Dakota village that they might run across over in the vicinity of Lake Traverse.

They probably didn't know much about the geography of the region but expected to prowl around on the sly, and when they found a village or camp, they would lie in wait until a good chance presented itself and make an attack and kill as many as possible and take home a bunch of scalps.

Somewhere along Lake Traverse, they found a village of Dakota, which they attacked and quite a battle ensued, but the defenders of the village were able to beat them off, and they retreated. Probably there were a few killed on both sides, but no details were known.

The Mandan took flight toward the north rather than toward the west, where their homes were. All the warriors of the village immediately took up arms, and without any war party formalities, they started in pursuit of the Mandan.

The war party may have been worn out after their long journey from the Missouri River, but the Dakota were fresh and rested, and so they had the advantage over their enemies in physical condition. The Mandan were unable to outdistance the Dakota in their flight, and so, seeing that they could not make their escape, they decided to make a stand someplace if they found a suitable location.

They went toward the north, and someplace along the Red River they found along the bluffs a place where the rains and water had washed out a very deep, large gully. This they thought would be a good place to make a stand and fight it out with the Sioux. As the war party was numerous, they seemed to have confidence in themselves.

Grandpa Fred heard this story from Lazarus Skyman, who was the son of Maȟpiyawicaśta or Cloudman, a Mdewakaŋtoŋwaŋ leader. Skyman was born in 1840 and died in 1927 at Pejuhutazizi. In the 1918 census that Grandpa Fred sent to the Pipestone superintendent, he is listed as seventy-eight and single. His daughter Emma, age thirty-five, was married to Joseph Redday.

They had no weapons other than their Native arms—bows and arrows and clubs and spears. The Dakota also were armed similarly except one man who had a flintlock gun. This, of course, was something he had gotten from some white trader.

The Mandan took refuge in this gully which they had found and determined to make a stand there. They had very good protection in this washout, as it was deep and the sides were steep—but they could not fight much, as the sides were too steep to climb up, so they could not shoot over the top, and also the Sioux could not creep up and peek over the edge of the gully to shoot without too much risk of a volley of arrows from down below.

Things stood this way for some time. It was a stalemate, and neither side could get a shot at the other. The Mandan did not dare to try to run away, as they seemed to be worn out from traveling and were no match for the Sioux, who were fresh from home.

The Mandan were huddled together at the head of the gully with steep banks for protection. But below the gully, out on the flat bottomland and in full view of the whole length of the gully but out of bowshot, a very large tree stood.

After some time, the Sioux sized up the situation and decided that that large tree would be of much advantage to them. Those with bows could not use it, but this one man with a flintlock gun, seeing his chance, kept out of bowshot and went down below and crept up under shelter of the tree and took position there. He had a full view of the whole length of the gully, and the Mandan were huddled together in a group at the upper end under the steep banks.

Here the warrior with the gun had the whole war party at his mercy. He was out of bowshot from them, but they were in range of gunshot from him. He sat there and leisurely loaded his gun and took a shot just as he pleased, and they had no means of escape. The main war party had them herded into a helpless bunch while the man with the gun leisurely took a shot at them whenever he got his gun loaded and picked them off just as he pleased.

This continued until they were all killed except two or three. These were allowed to escape so they could go home with the news of the disaster.

As this one man received credit for killing the whole war party, he was entitled to wear a feather for each one he had killed. Necessarily, he wore a great many feathers and received the name of Many Feathers or Ornaments. What his real name may have been was never told.

But for all the honors he received for this great exploit in war, in the end he came to his death in a most unexpected manner.

Sometime after the above events took place, this man was traveling around the country, and he made a visit at one of the Indian agencies which the government had established a short time since. There he saw many things that were curious to him, and he took great delight in sightseeing.

Sometimes now we hear of some soldier returning home from Korea or World War II after being in the thick of the fighting over there and being in terrific danger in combat, only to be killed here at home in some fool automobile accident. The same kind of an unexpected death awaited Many Feathers, but who could have foretold it?

During his visit at the agency, he went down one day to the blacksmith shop which the government maintained for the Indians. It was quite a sight to him to see the men making things of iron, to see how they could heat the iron red hot and beat it with a hammer into various shapes and make tools of it or make horseshoes and nail them onto the hooves of horses.

As was the custom of the time, no one ever went anyplace without his weapons. He still had his flintlock gun and took that with him to the blacksmith shop, and also it was loaded.

He was standing in the blacksmith shop watching a man beat a piece of red-hot iron into some kind of a tool, and the sparks were flying all around inside the building. No one suspected what those sparks could do. Intently watching the workman, he rested the butt of his gun on the floor and rested his chin over the muzzle of the gun.

In a flintlock gun there is a small pan at the back end of the gun barrel which has a little powder in it. To discharge the gun, a spark from the flint goes into the powder in this little pan and ignites it, and from this pan, a small hole leads to the real charge of powder down in the barrel behind the bullet.

He was leisurely standing this way watching the sparks fly and thinking how wonderful it was now they could make things of iron in this way. Suddenly, one of the red-hot sparks flew into the ignition pan at the back end of the gun barrel, causing the gun to discharge and sending the bullet up through his head and killing him instantly.

As a sequel to the above narrative, the following account is told among the Mdewakaŋtoŋwaŋ or Santee people of Minnesota.

In the 1850s, when the government had established the Lower Agency along the Minnesota River below where Redwood Falls now stands, there was also a blacksmith shop for the Indians. The blacksmith was a French Canadian by the name of Campbell.

One day, some Indians were visiting the shop, and one had a flintlock gun, all loaded, too. He rested the butt of the gun on the ground, and the muzzle was up against the lower part of his face or his neck.

A spark from the anvil flew into the ignition pan of the gun, causing it to discharge, killing the man instantly. The blacksmith became afraid and feared that he might be blamed for this man's death, and fearing a reprisal he ran away and left his agency job, but he still continued companionship with the Indians.

He seemed to have gone to Manitoba, Canada, where he came in contact with the Indians from Minnesota after their exodus from their homeland. There, he married an Indian woman and raised a family.

A son of his named John Campbell afterward came back to this country and married a woman of the Sisseton Reservation in South Dakota. About the year 1907, he lived with his family near the town of Peever, South Dakota.

One summer evening, some white men took some intoxicating liquor to his place. A drinking party took place. Before morning, John Campbell was dead, supposedly as a result of the drinking.

Mato

A young man once was in mourning for the death of some relative, and after some time, he started out on the war path all alone. He went west.

After some days traveling, he came upon a large village of the enemy. He was noted for his swiftness of foot. He went upon a hill and was watching the village, expecting to find a chance to kill an enemy, when he saw three men watching him in turn.

He did not know what to do. After a little while, he saw the men looking at him again, but this time there were only two, so he knew that one had gone back to the village to summon up a war party to come and attack him. He thought his chances were very poor now, so he tried to run away and take refuge somewhere. A few miles back, he had passed a large grove of big trees, and he thought that if he could get into that grove he would stand a show.

There was a long ravine that led in a roundabout manner out on the prairie and then turned and led back to the grove. Taking to this ravine, he ran with all the speed he could gather, but before he reached the grove, he could hear the war party thundering along over the prairie after him.

He now renewed his efforts, and finally he reached the grove, but the war party was now not very far behind him. He ran to the center of the grove and accidentally there he found a grizzly bear's den. Outside this den a large basswood tree had fallen, and there was quite a little room under the old log. The moss had grown over this log and hung down on both sides, so he crawled in under this and was well sheltered from view.

Pretty soon, the war party came crashing up through the woods and tracked him to the bear's den. They surrounded the bear's den, expecting to be able to kill him soon.

As it happened, the bear was at home. The warrior under the log supposed that they had found him and was expecting them to come up to the log to kill him, so he got his gun ready and also his bow and arrow ready to shoot and kill one if possible. But instead of going to the log, they thought he had taken refuge in the bear's den.

When the bear saw the war party, he supposed of course that they had come for him, and he soon made a sortie on them. He killed one of the men and chewed his throat badly and dragged him back into his den.

The war party seemed to be powerless to do anything against him. The bear kept making sortie after sortie, until he had killed seven men of the war party and brought them back into his den.

Then the war party thought that it was a very unfortunate piece of business, and an old man among them that was somewhat smarter than the rest saw through their misfortune, and he yelled out in a loud voice, "All this is a very unlucky piece of business. We thought we had chased a man up here into this bear's den, but instead of that, it was some supernatural being, for he has turned himself into a bear here and has killed seven of our chiefs. We had better withdraw now and save ourselves further misfortunes." When he got through with his speech, they withdrew and started off through the forest toward home.

The man under the log did not know what to do. The bear might find him now and kill him, but he patiently waited to see what was going to happen.

About the time the war party had got to the edge of the woods, the bear started out after them. The warrior waited until he was sure that the bear had got out of sight and hearing. Then he got up as quickly as possible and scalped the whole seven warriors that the bear had killed and started toward home as fast as he could.

He traveled as speedily as possible until he was entirely out of reach of the war party and then took it a little slower. He came to a swamp and waded out in the middle and got on a rock among the rushes, and there he prepared the seven scalps by soaking them in the water and rubbing off the flesh that adhered.

After he got through there, he started along toward home again, and after some time he came to a tract of woods. Here he passed through and came to a rotten log. With the rotten wood he dried the scalps and prepared them some more.

Then he started out toward home again, and when he got near home, he stopped in some woods and cut some vines down that he made circles out of to stretch the scalps in. There he fastened some sticks to use for handles, and then he twisted wild hemp bark into little strings, and with these he laced the scalps into the circles of wood. When he had the whole seven all ready, he had quite a pack.

Then he went home and walked into the courtyard of the village. Someone soon recognized him, and a herald soon began calling out, "The young man that started out on the war path all along has returned. He has killed an enemy and came home." When the full news was known about his bringing home seven scalps, it was looked upon as a most remarkable piece of warfare.

The Warrior Who Lost His Brother

The following was told by some of the old men of the Ascension district of the old Sisseton and Wahpeton reservation of South Dakota—Wasu, Tasiŋte, Okiha, Oieśica, Cataka Ihduze, Ohaŋna, David Amos.

In the old times, sometimes two men would become much attached to each other. In fact, such attachments are something that would be impossible to find among white people today. Sometimes two friends or two brothers or two brother-in-laws would become so attached to each other that they would risk anything in the world for each other, and if one should get killed in war, nothing could avenge his death but the killing of an enemy. This was sometimes done or attempted in the most hazardous manner imaginable.

A young man was once very much attached to his brother-in-law. His brother-in-law was killed by Chippeway; he went into deep mourning, and nothing could pacify him but the killing of an enemy.

Not long after this, a Chippeway war party of five members came to make war on the Dakota. They dug a kind of breastwork up on a hill not far from the Dakota village and, there, waited for a chance to make an attack. Several different warriors went out singularly to attack them but were always killed, as the Chippeway had the advantage entirely.

After a number had been killed in this way, the relatives of our hero thought they would try his prowess. Now, among the Indians they say that there is no mark in the world so hard to hit in shooting as a naked man running a zigzag manner in an oblique direction. (Such tactics were used in the First World War by the Allies fighting in France and Germany.) If he keeps running and jumping and throwing himself first down on the ground and getting up quickly and jumping from right to left, he stands a very good show of not being hit.

So, they took the young man and gave him no weapons except a butcher knife in each hand. They instructed him how to dodge their shots and then started him for the Chippeway. When he got in gunshot of them, they began shooting at him and he began running and dodging them. They all shot about the same time.

When their guns were all empty, then running as fast as he could, he attacked them hand to hand in their breastworks before they had time to reload their guns. He jumped in among them and stabbed right and left with all his might and killed the whole five right there.

Of course, this act put him in high estimation in the village, and he was very much respected.

Story of a Young Brave

A young man was once gambling with some others, and he was very unfortunate. His medicine was not strong, and after he had been playing for some time, he lost everything he had, even most of his clothing. He was with a large party on a buffalo hunt somewhere east of the Missouri River, and not a great distance from the Minataree Indians (one of the three tribes of the Fort Berthold Reservation).

After he had lost everything he had, he went back to his lodge, which he occupied with an only sister, although he had two brothers in the village. His sister, among other property, possessed some elk teeth, earrings, and a bear claw necklace. He asked her for these, saying that he had lost everything and wished for something more to stake on the game. She refused his request, saying that gambling was not a good pastime and that she didn't care to use up her property on such business.

He was very angry at her and sat in silence for some time. Then he took off the last vestige of clothing he wore except his breechcloth and said to her, "In the future, you will remember me, but you can have that necklace and earrings for your brother in place of me." Then he combed his hair nicely and painted the part in it and painted his face nicely and left the lodge.

He passed through the village and departed toward the west. By this time, some of his other relatives had heard what had happened, and they followed him out of the village and offered him all sorts of presents and clothing of the finest kinds, saying that he could have them and do as he pleased with them, but he turned a deaf ear to them and went on his way almost absolutely naked.

Minataree is another name for the Hidatsa, who are part of the Mandan Hidatsa Arikara Nation, also known as the Three Affiliated Tribes.

Some of the people followed him for a half a day or so, but their entreaties were of no avail. After traveling something like two days, he arrived pretty close to the Minataree village.

One morning, as he lay on the prairie after a heavy rain, he saw a dark object in the distance. He lay flat on the ground, concealing himself among the sagebrush, and watched this object. It turned out to be an Indian warrior in full dress, carrying a gun and bow and arrows, besides his clothing, which was of the finest make.

This party came up onto a small rise of ground and took a position there and then dropped out of sight among the sagebrush. A small ravine separated their two locations.

He thought to himself, "I am pretty swift, and if I get up and run as fast as I can down into this ravine, I don't think I'll be seen." Following his thought by act, he got up and ran as fast as he could down into the ravine, and from there he crawled through the sagebrush up where the gaily bedecked warrior had taken up his position. He found him lying in the sagebrush, sound asleep, snoring.

Having no weapons of any kind, he was at a loss as to what to do. There were no stones on the ground near, so he got up and ran on a hill as fast as he could, looking for a stone which might assist as a weapon for him.

After some little time of hunting, he found a stone about the size of a man's two fists. With this he struck the warrior a hard blow directly on the forehead. It took effect, for the warrior groaned and straightened out on the ground. One more blow to make sure, and then he proceeded to dismantle his foe. He took off all the clothing that the warrior wore and all the weapons and his scalp.

He then started for home as swift as he possibly could, for he was afraid that this warrior was only one of a large party, and when they found him dead, they would start in pursuit. The grass being wet after the rain, his track was very easy to follow in the grass. But even if the grass was not wet, the Native people could follow trails that could not be seen by an inexperienced eye. He knew this and depended on his speed to be able to reach home and give the alarm about the war party.

He reached home safely and spread the alarm about the war party and knew that they would be able to follow his trail on the prairie. As proof that he was not mistaken about the war party, he had that scalp and all the costume and weapons that he had taken from the warrior he had slain.

Preparations were immediately made to give the war party a warm reception. All the old people and women and children were hustled out of the camp and hid in the brush and small timber along a creek near the camp, and all the able-bodied warriors, fully armed, remained at the camp to do battle with the enemy.

Sometime later, the enemy war party arrived and a fierce battle took place, but no details of the fight were given. At any rate, the people were well warned, and there was no surprise attack.

The Bear Story

When I was a small boy, there used to be a man in our camp who was a very industrious hunter, and we small boys, and the grown people, too, thought a good deal of him and depended much upon him, as he brought a great deal of meat to camp. Come to think of it, I guess you here will recognize him in a way. He was a brother of Oġaġadaŋ, and he was related to me, being a cousin of my mother.

As usual, one morning, he started out from camp to hunt at a lake which lay entirely surrounded by prairie. As he approached the lake, he saw a flock of ducks close to the shore and thought that he would be able to crawl up through the high grass and get a shot at them. He had a muzzle-loading gun of very large bore, possibly a ten-gauge.

As he started crawling through the grass, suddenly the ducks seemed to get excited and appeared to see something on the shore and started toward the middle of the lake. Wondering what the cause of the excitement was, he began watching the shore of the lake as he crawled and presently saw a grizzly bear waddling along the shore. The bear was too close at hand to think of running away, and so he thought to do his best and hold his own.

Lying in the grass, he drew the load of shot from the gun and put

The speaker in this story is not Grandpa Fred. He is retelling a story he heard from someone else long ago.

in a couple of large slugs and rammed them down and then lay in wait behind a bunch of tall grass. His idea was to get a close shot and try to break a bone of one of the bear's legs and cripple him very seriously. A shot through the body would have no immediate effect, and the bear could easily overtake a man and kill him, especially if he was maddened by a wound.

The bear worked leisurely along the shore, tearing up the trash that drifted in and now and then finding a lizard which he ate. Bears have eating habits something like hogs. In fact, a bear is something like a hog in build as well as in habits.

The hunter, not knowing what to do, was bound to make the best out of a tight place. He watched the bear as he threw the drift trash right and left and high above his head as he hunted for delicious morsels of food. By this time, he was about opposite to the hunter but on the edge of the water, while the hunter lay behind a bunch of tall grass, a short distance back of the water.

Suddenly, the bear's attention was attracted to something a few feet back from the water, where he seemed to find something to call his attention. Then the hunter noticed a slight hillock just back from the shore, and a skunk stood there facing the bear.

He waited anxiously to see what happened. Suddenly, the skunk threw his scent and a yellow cloud which enveloped the bear. The skunk had made a true shot. For a few seconds, no results showed, but suddenly, as the scent penetrated and took effect on the bear's eyes, he gave an awful howl and started rubbing his eyes with his paws, standing up. It might be well to say here that the scent thrown by a skunk is one of the most painful things imaginable if it reaches the eyes of either man or beast.

Now or never, while the bear was blinded by the scent of the skunk, the hunter jumped up and ran to the bear. Jamming the muzzle of the gun in the breast, he discharged it, and the bear tumbled over and rolled around some and was dead.

Possibly if it had not been for the skunk, he might not have lived to tell the story.

The bear meat made a big addition to the provisions in camp.

Itesaŋyapi

This story my mom told me. There was a root medicine man called Doctor Quinn who walked from reservation to reservation doctoring the people. He seemed to do the four Dakota communities and perhaps others, but I am not sure. This was before Upper Sioux was established, so I suppose he went to the two villages in this area, Ḣeku (Below the Hill) and Kaḣmiŋ (Bend in the River). My mom said he had this extraordinary ability to show up when he was most needed without being called. His Indian name was Itesaŋyapi, which meant something like His Face Is Gray or Made Gray. Of course, his patients were poor and could not pay him. So, they fed him good. He reportedly would put too much salt on his food, and he would taste his food and say, "Oh, this is too salty. Can I get some more to make it less salty?" Supposedly this was how he got his Dakota name.

Indian Ball Players

A couple of years ago at Ḣe Sapa Powwow, a friend and I had a good remembrance conversation about the Indian fast-pitch teams from the Sisseton Reservation. Oh, there were some good ball players coming out of there. One time, Dad took me to a tournament of the Sisseton teams which was played at the field in Sisseton. I suppose we came up to watch Upper Sioux play. I was always interested in the pitchers, and at that time, the one to watch was Tom Big Talk—could he throw the ball. Then later, at our powwow, we had a softball tournament and Eggleston (aka Prairie Island) showed up with their pitcher, Gordy Campbell—another great pitcher. This was all in the '50s, early '60s. I was too young to play but loved fast-pitch. All others played kittenball.

Weasel

I was thinking about a relative (in the Indian way). Weasel was my grandpa and grandma's grandson, but also in an Indian way. He was enrolled at the Prairie Band Potawatomi Reservation in Kansas but raised up here in Pejuhutazizi. It seemed Weasel (whose real name was Vernon, but everybody called him Weasel) did not want to go to school in Granite, and he kept skipping school, so the plan was for him to go to Flandreau Indian School. Grandpa and Grandma drove him down to Flandreau to the boarding school. However, he decided he did not want to attend there, either, so he caught the Great Northern freight home and was sitting in Grandpa's yard when they returned. He beat them home because my grandpa's top speed was thirty miles an hour, since he came from the horse-and-buggy days. Weasel eventually joined the Marines and went to Korea to fight. He came back quite a hero, and I remember his stories of fighting the Chinese army. I used to hang out with a lot of older people and listen to their stories. One who also went to Korea said he didn't even know where Korea was. Let us hope our young don't have to repeat this part of history.

Stories Reconcile

Sometimes stories have the ability to reconcile painful events, perhaps of loved ones long gone, ushering in much-needed compassion. Stories also have the power to reclaim and reconnect a shared past to a collective future.

Waṡicuŋ

Along the Mississippi River, where it forms the boundary between Minnesota and Wisconsin, there were some white people living there, about the year 1850.

On the Wisconsin side, there were legitimate settlers and farmers of a kind, but if any were on the Minnesota side, they were not legitimate settlers but were squatters living there by farming.

There may be a tale among the descendants of any such settlers of a small boy who disappeared one winter and was never heard of again.

After the Treaty of 1837 and before the Treaty of 1851, the lands east of the Mississippi in this area became part of Wisconsin Territory and were opened to white settlers; lands west of the river had not been ceded.

He probably was given up for lost and supposed to be dead, as the weather was cold and there were wild animals aplenty that could have eaten him up.

In about the year mentioned, the Santee or Mdewakaŋtoŋwaŋ Sioux still held that part of Minnesota along the Mississippi River. At one of their camps along the river, one winter day, a couple of women had been cooking hulled corn or hominy or lyed corn. In making this article of food, the Indian corn such as they raise is cooked with ashes until the outer covering of the kernel is loose. Then it is put in a mesh bag woven out of fibers of basswood bark and taken to a stream of water. A hole was cut in the ice and the whole sack was immersed in the water and the ashes washed out of the corn, after which it was cooked with meat for eating.

These two women had cooked their corn and taken it to the river to wash it. They took their time and worked leisurely. Naturally, they were on the lookout. No Indian is ever so absorbed in his occupation but what he or she is constantly on the lookout for anything that might be sinister or otherwise. During their work, one of the women looked across the ice and saw a small child walking toward them. Who could it be? They watched the child approaching and then saw that he was a little white boy.

Where he came from no one knew, as there were no settlements of white people near that location known to the Indians. He must have traveled quite a distance. As to whether he came from across the river or across a bend of the river, the account does not make it plain, but at any rate he came across the ice to where the women were washing their corn. He seemed to be hungry, as he picked up and ate some of the kernels of corn which had fallen on the ice.

The women could not talk with him, as he was a white boy—and then, too, he was too small to talk intelligently. When they got ready and went back to their camp, he followed them. He being a child and cold winter weather, the only thing they could do was care for him as best they could, which might have been as well or better than how some of the early settlers lived.

Maybe they expected someone to come looking for the child. Probably it was a lucky thing for the Indians that no one came to their camp looking for the child. If that child had been found in the Indian camp under those conditions, some hot-headed official or army officer might have accused them of kidnapping and demanded hostages be delivered regardless of all reasonable explanations, which might have led to hostilities. There was no white settlement known in that location, and as he had chosen these women to be his guardian, there was nothing they could do but take care of him.

He lived with these women, and one took him as her son and spoke of him as such. He lived the life of any of the Indian boys of the time and in all respects and deportment was Indian, although he knew that he was not really Indian. Whether he knew that from being told by others, or did he have a faint memory of being among white people? He had one distinguished mark, and that was he was cross-eyed. Everyone who had ever seen him or knew him always remarked about his cross-eye.

As he grew larger, the tribe emigrated west and settled along the Minnesota River near Redwood Falls, Minnesota. In that location an agency was established, and this boy grew up near there. Here at what was called the Lower Agency, the Indians had many dealings with white people. Part of these dealings were with officials, many of whom were avowed enemies of the Indians, and other dealings were with the traders, who were always unscrupulous in their dealings.

Sometimes tribal members out on hunting expeditions came up missing, and in northern Iowa a whole family was murdered by a white man. This was a well-established fact and known to many. When a complaint against this act was lodged at the agency, the agent only laughed it off. Such treatment did not set well with the tribe. Finally becoming exasperated with such shabby treatment, in August 1862, they rebelled against all the injustices committed against them and a sort of war ensued.

After the signing of the Treaty of 1851, Dakota bands were required to move to reservations along the Minnesota River, where they lived until 1862. The Sisitoŋwaŋ and Waȟpetoŋwaŋ were at Upper Sioux Agency; the Mdewakaŋtoŋwaŋ and Waȟpekute were at Lower Sioux Agency.

The murder of this family in Iowa was the cause of the Spirit Lake "Massacre": trader Henry Lott murdered Iŋkpaduta's brother Siŋtomniduta, his wife, and their five children in 1854. Instead of seeking justice, the prosecuting attorney displayed Siŋtomniduta's head on a pole outside his home. There was even further provocation, and Iŋkpaduta finally attacked.

After a few skirmishes, the Indians were driven from their homes and a great many were taken prisoners, and among them was this white boy. These prisoners were all kept in some hastily built log barracks at Mankato, Minnesota. The only heat, although it was winter, were open fires, and they had straw on the ground for beds.

Finally, the day for the execution came. A squad of soldiers went through the barracks gathering up those that were to be hanged.

Now it happened that this white boy was named Wašicuŋ, which means a white man. Also among the prisoners was a mixed-blood who was rather light complexioned, also called Wašicuŋ.

The soldiers passed through the barracks with an officer who had a list of names of the condemned, and when he read off a name the victim was taken off. When he read the name Wašicuŋ, the intended victim was that mixed-blood man, but he did not answer. He just lay still under his blanket on the straw.

Then the white boy, knowing that was his name, said to the other prisoners, "I might as well get it over with. Here I am suffering under all these hardships and have no relations, and no one cares for me. I might as well get it over with." So, he arose from his bed of straw and was taken with the other victims and hanged.

After the hanging, the executioners found out that they had hanged a white man, one of their own people, but because their rabid prejudice against the Indians had backfired, they kept it quiet, and it never was told among the white people. Although a few knew it and all the Indians knew it.

Afterward the Indians always poked gibes at the white people for hanging one of their own number, thinking he was Indian. Did the real parents of that boy ever know what became of him? What would they have thought to know that he was hanged?

All the Indians knew it.

Aftereffects

As a youngster I heard that Isabelle Roberts, Maza Okiye Wiŋ, re-fused to eat eggs because of those Dakota men who stole eggs from that wašicuŋ family in 1862, which eventually sparked the Dakota War of that year and brought on all the misery for Dakota people. I guess that must have been her little protest of how an insignificant event can cause such turmoil and tragedy.

• • • •

When I was young, I thought all of us Dakota participated in the war, but Dad told me no, that the Sisitoŋwaŋ and Wahpetoŋwaŋ did not. Initially I found that hard to believe, because we lost our reservation, too, and were exiled out of Minnesota. I often refer to Tiwakaŋ's Narrative, and that is chock-full of information. He states that the Mdewakaŋtoŋwaŋ started the war without consulting the other bands, and if they did, the Sisitoŋwaŋ probably would have gone to war also. Now he says that the Sisitoŋwaŋ and Wahpe-toŋwaŋ suffered the same fate. I understand that tension because I felt that same growing up.

• • • •

"Tehika do" is how Dad described the experiences of his mother Sagadašiŋ or Sarah Renville on that march to the internment camp at Fort Snelling in 1862. Tehika means difficult, hard. She was three or four years old. My grandmother's father, Tiwakaŋ, Gabriel Renville, wrote in his Narrative that every morning they woke up to someone else dying in their tipi and having to deal with that. I wonder what they did with the bodies since it was winter and very difficult to dig a grave. I wonder if they put them on a scaffold and took the bones down in the spring.

Both of Dad's parents lived through the 1862 war and its tragic aftermath, yet the stories Dad told were all from his mother. Yet his dad, Philip LaBatte, had a much more tragic experience in that his father, Francois LaBatte, half Dakota, half French, was killed in the war. Obviously, Philip chose not to speak of his experience, at least to Dad. Was it too terrible to speak of, I wonder?

• • • •

Walter LaBatte as a baby with his sister Maude and parents Sarah Renville LaBatte and Philip LaBatte, 1900.

Back in the '70s, when I did family history—and, in a larger sense, Dakota history—Mom warned me about uncovering unpleasant things, not only about wašicuŋ but about other bands, and maybe it should be best to let sleeping dogs lie. I already knew what she was referring to, because I always felt that tension between Mdewakaŋtoŋwaŋ and their allies the Waȟpekute and we Sisitoŋwaŋ. I always knew what side of the fence I was on. I suspect the Sisitoŋwaŋ blamed the others for the war and for losing their reservation, and perhaps the Mdewakaŋtoŋwaŋ blamed the Sisitoŋwaŋ for not joining in the chaos. Maybe the younger generation is not aware of this, and so maybe Mother got her wish, but should we forget history or rather learn to face it?

• • • •

Tiyotipi has been translated as Soldiers' Lodge, wherein certain strategies were discussed by the chiefs and headmen. When a Tiyotipi was called, the woman who was the best tipi maker was asked to provide her tipi for the meeting. These meetings were usually called to discuss tribal business, such as buffalo-hunt strategy and other issues that needed to be addressed. After the issue(s) were thoroughly discussed, the group had to reach a unanimous decision, as all needed to be behind the decision. Sometimes it would take days to accomplish this. After the decision was made, the eyapaha would go out to camp announcing the decision. In Tiwakaŋ's Narrative, he talks about the Sisitoŋwaŋ people calling a Tiyotipi in that fateful summer of 1862. After the start of the war, some Sisitoŋwaŋ were captured and held hostage by the Mdewakaŋtoŋwaŋ soldiers, and among the hostages was Tiwakaŋ's sister. So, the Sisitoŋwaŋ were wondering if the Mdewakaŋtoŋwaŋ were going to attack them; thus the Tiyotipi was called west of Riggs's mission. They were going to arm themselves for protection and demand the hostages' release. Some of Little Crow's soldiers arrived and made a show of hostilities but backed down after the Sisitoŋwaŋ showed their resolve to fight. Years ago, one of the old guys here described that area to me where the Tiyotipi was. At the time, I really did not know what he was referring to. It seemed to be in a field where I picked rocks when I was a teenager for the wašicuŋ farmer called Caske Hanska, which is west of the tribe's Prairie's Edge RV park, on the south side of the road. This is some history we ignore, but I know it was the basis for the tension between the bands in my youth.

The Battle of the Little Big Horn, 1876

Here and there, anyone hears details of events that have taken place in the past, and very often those details are something that is not in line with the accepted version of those events.

In regard to the Custer fight out on the Little Big Horn—or, as some versions have it, the Greasy Grass—an old man named Izuza, or Grindstone, told about what he saw of the fight. He took no part in it. He said:

A very large village of us were camped in a circle, and my camp was on the west side of the encampment. The people were not thinking of a fight but were minding their own business and looking for buffalo, as that was their main living. No one was expecting anything serious to happen that day, only wishing for a chance to have a big buffalo hunt so that the people could have plenty to eat.

I was at home, not expecting anything out of the ordinary camp life

The Battle of Greasy Grass, known to whites as the Battle of Little Bighorn or Custer's Last Stand, took place on the Crow Reservation in Montana Territory on June 25–26, 1876. The 7th US Cavalry, under General George Armstrong Custer, attacked a camp of Lakota, Northern Cheyenne, and Arapaho people that vastly outnumbered the soldiers. In the battle that followed, Native forces killed 268 of the 700 troops and severely wounded 55 others. News of the event reached the East Coast on July 4, 1876, the centennial of the Declaration of Independence.

to happen, when suddenly down at the east end of the encampment an army of white men appeared, marching from the east.

They halted and blew their bugles and stood there a short time and then proceeded toward the center of the camp. After marching a short distance, they stopped again and blew their bugles. Then they proceeded again toward the center of the camp. I didn't know what it was all about and did not know what was going to happen. Suddenly, fighting began—our warriors had attacked them, as they had invaded our camp for no reason. And we were peacefully hunting for a buffalo herd. The fight lasted for only a short time, possibly half an hour, and then it was over, and all the soldiers had been killed.

That was one man's observation of the fight.

Another man recounting details of that fight said: After the battle was over, we ransacked all the property of the dead soldiers, and among their possessions we found a lot of little green pieces of paper. We didn't know what those green papers were, so we burnt them. Afterward, we found out that those pieces of paper were money, but we had burnt them all up.

Another man recounting events in connection with that battle told the following: We were encamped there, not expecting anything serious to happen, when all of a sudden that army of white men for no reason at all invaded our camp. The chiefs and headmen held a hasty council of war to decide what to do in self-defense. They decided to attack them and not let them get by with their uncalled-for arrogance. "How shall we fight them?" they said.

Someone suggested that they circle around them on their ponies, at the same time fighting them. Then someone suggested that they ride ponies right in among the soldiers and cut the ranks all to pieces.

The latter operation was decided upon as being the best way to fight them. So that was what they did, and we all know the results. Custer's whole army was killed in the fight—no survivors.

Name Changing

At one time the Indian Bureau got the idea of straightening out the names of the Indians. A great many of them were translations of the old tribal names. Some were very clumsy and some rather vulgar.

Among the Dakota the missionaries had baptized a great many, giving them English or Bible names. The descendants of such generally took the baptismal name of the father as a last or family name.

In the case of your family, the name Amos was taken as a family name. The Indian Bureau gave Charles Eastman the job of correcting the tribal names. He made a lot of changes in the names of the people. He went from one agency to another and spent several months at each place correcting the names. In the case of your family, he discarded the Amos and used a translation of your great-grandfather's name and called your family Red Lodge. No one ever knew when he was at Sisseton Agency doing this work. He used only the records at the agency,

Dr. Charles Alexander Eastman, Ohiyesa, was born in 1858. His father was Wakaŋhdi Ota. His mother, Winona or Nancy, was the only child of Wakhaŋ Inažiŋ Wiŋ (Stands Sacred) and Seth Eastman, an army officer at Fort Snelling. Ohiyesa grew up with relatives who fled to Canada in 1862, then was reunited with his father when he was fifteen. He attended Dartmouth College and Boston University, becoming one of the country's first Native physicians in 1890. He served as the agency physician at Pine Ridge and Crow Creek Reservations, caring for those injured in the Wounded Knee Massacre in 1890. In 1903, he accepted a presidential appointment to revise the Sioux allotment rolls, which involved assigning family names; this work was intended to protect property rights of heirs. He later became a leader in the YWCA and wrote eleven popular books.

which were very often incorrect and incomplete—especially at Sisseton Agency, as that building was once burned down with all the records. He made a big job of it and even wrote a magazine article about it. At any rate, he put the name Red Lodge on all of your mother's family and changed the names of a great many of the other people, but almost no tribal members ever knew anything about his correcting the names of the people. All those records are packed away in the Indian office, and no one ever pays any attention to them and very few knew that such records exist.

Tribal Governance

There is a certain amount of criticism of the Indian Reorganization Act of the 1930s. Some of it concerns the imposition or the encouragement of a democratic government in tribal affairs. I suspect there were some tribes that had a traditional chief government, but many had long lost that type of government. I think about Gabriel Renville being the last of the chiefs. The positive which I see in the IRA was the halting of the allotments era. When Pejuhutazizi was formed, all land was held by the tribe, and only land assignments were given. Thus, no mortgaged property was lost, and halting allotments ended that threat.

Before World War II, the Nazis referred to the "Jewish problem." I remember in the '50s, the US government referred to the "Indian problem." I didn't know I was a problem. The US government solved or attempted to solve the "problem" by termination and relocation. Kind of like a "national emergency." Our Pejuhutazizi Reservation, aka Upper Sioux, was on the chopping block.

Indian termination, the federal policy lasting from the 1940s to the 1960s, was a set of laws that forced assimilation, ended treaty obligations, closed reservations, and simply declared that a tribe no longer existed. The Indian Relocation Act of 1956 paid for people to leave reservations and move to cities, where they were to receive vocational training.

This government proposal to terminate the Dakota reservations in Minnesota entailed giving assignment owners title to their land— taking it out of common ownership, paying property taxes, and of course giving the ability to sell. That would have just broken up our reservation and ended our government-to-government relationship. I remember we were all in turmoil here about the potential loss, and we were nearly 100 percent opposed except for one individual. We lucked out because the State of Minnesota realized their expenses might increase, and they didn't want the responsibility.

• • • •

Back in the '70s, when I was chairman, I dealt with the political strife often present in tribal politics. Families who were out of power almost immediately caused strife for the families in power, and the roles were reversed when they got back in. There never seemed to be anyone concerned with the welfare of the entire tribe, not just with taking care of their own families. I studied ways of doing away with that and so read up on how we governed ourselves in the past. There was not a whole lot of info available, but what I did find was that in the past, every family or family group was represented in council so that no one felt left out, as it was in my chairman's days. Only the families could remove their representatives—not council. Also, it took 100 percent approval to pass any council action so that there were no saboteurs of council action. Imagine the persuasion abilities needed. Knowing my tribe, I recognized those family connections, and I could see that it was possible to form a council with five or six council positions representing all the families at Pejuhutazizi. I presented my view to the rest of council but received lukewarm to no backing. I could see where it could be done in a small reservation.

I deal with tribal politics now by just ignoring it—it keeps me sane and with my peace and serenity intact.

Land Claim Settlements

In the 1940s, the US government started an attempt to make recompense for the broken treaties, establishing the Indian Claims Commission. So, in the '60s, when the land claim settlements were being discussed in Dakota country in Minnesota, all the elders of that time

> Marvin Sonosky began representing tribal clients in the 1950s.
> In 1976, he founded the law firm that is now Sonosky, Chambers,
> Sachse, Endreson & Perry, LLP.

were talking about the government's offerings—six cents per acre
and no interest. Also discussed was how this money would be distributed. Of course, all the elders were fluent in Dakota, and most of the
talks were in Dakota, for it was easier for them to express themselves
in their first language. Oliver Sudden, this English term, per capita,
popped into the conversation. Woooh, where did this word come
from? Not even of English extraction but perhaps Latin. And our
Dakota elders were slinging around such a word! Nowadays, all Indians, not just Dakota, know that word, and it is tossed around in its
shortened version—per cap.

   Here is my recollection of that meeting to discuss the government's offering for the land settlement. In attendance was a rep from
the Sonosky law firm in Washington, DC, who came to present the
government's offer for us to discuss. They offered to pay what the
original terms were—some $6 million for our land in Minnesota, the
exact same terms from the 1851 and 1858 treaties, coming to pennies
per acre. This amount did not include any money for a hundred years
of interest. Some of the younger people were upset with the offer, and
my tahaŋśi asked, "Why do we have to always do what the government wants? We should hold out for a fairer deal." One of the elders
said that she has been waiting all her life for this and would accept
anything the government offered. This all took a good ten years
before the money was distributed, maybe $1,200 per capita. Unfor-
tunately, this kuŋśi died before she received any money.

Śiceca

Who all can remember the grade school and junior high taunts and
bullying? Perhaps by high school everyone matured, and it was no
longer a problem. I can remember the bullying and being called
squaw man. I complained to my mother, expecting her to go to the
principal or teacher. She didn't. She said that the poor kid probably
didn't know any better, in that his parents didn't know themselves

how to act respectfully. Kids can be lil' devils sometimes, and I don't see why some call them Wakaŋheża—the sacred beings. I like our Dakota name, Śiceca, inferring the naughtiness of kids. I suppose Wakaŋheża is referring to infants.

Institutional Racism

It seems like there are some who don't believe that there is something like institutional racism. I assure you that I have experienced it three times in my lifetime. This all came about studying history of the rural electrification movement of the 1930s. President Franklin Roosevelt was concerned that farmers had access to electricity in the country. I thought to myself, hmmm, I wonder why it took an extra thirty-some years for electricity to come to my reservation while all the farmers around us enjoyed it. Then I remember that we had no rural delivery of mail on my reservation, again until the late '50s. My grandfather lived off the reservation, and that's where we got our mail. A couple of years ago, I asked at the Granite Falls Post Office why that was so. The woman got embarrassed and pissed off that I brought up the subject. She justified it by saying that was federal land. I asked, "So, you would not deliver mail to a federal office?" And the last example of institutional racism was the lack of phone service until 1966. People on the reservation petitioned the phone company to provide service, but they would do it only if we cut the right-of-way through the trees. My dad and brother did that work. On second thought, there is one more example. We asked the phone service to bring in internet connections for our computers, but they declined. So, our tribe brought in our own broadband. Now tell me that institutional racism does not exist and never existed.

• • • •

During my working career, I was well aware of white privilege—I was the last carpenter hired in the spring and the first laid off in the fall. I never let it bother me, never saw it as a roadblock, but rather looked at it as a challenge. I knew that it would be useless to complain about it or to even file a complaint, so I learned to work harder than my white neighbor. And because I constantly had to look for work with other companies, I learned a great many different and better techniques to accomplish the tasks assigned. So, all this paid off later—I found myself in a spot where the company I worked for needed me more than I needed them, as the union treasured my work record and always found work for me. In effect, I used that discrimination to my advantage. Only in retirement have I discovered that I shouldn't have had to get through that. I was a competent union worker from the start and should have been treated as such.

Owaŋgwaśte Wokaġa—Making Beauty

Addiction was a tough thing to get over. I got into it really hard. I have said many times that there are two routes to sobriety—the judge or the doctor. I was drinking for five years and ended up in the hospital with pancreatitis. The doctor told me this could kill me. I remembered what my mother said to me: "Super, if you want to quit drinking, ask Wakaŋtaŋka. He can do anything if you ask him." That sounded pretty out of this world. But nothing else was working, and I knew I was headed to the hospital, so I did what my mom told me to do. It felt kind of good; I felt relieved. I made a bargain with Wakaŋtaŋka: if you heal me so I don't have to go to the hospital, I'll quit. I kept praying, going back to my Dakota ways. Praying, praying, praying. That was a tough period in my life. Had I not sobered up, I wouldn't even be here. I would have been dead long time ago. I wouldn't have been able to express myself through art.

The mind is very powerful; it can take you to heaven or hell. I was in hell for a long time and never want to go back there. There's a lot of addictions out there. There's judgment looking outside of yourself, judgment you see in other people. If you keep denying, you can't fix things in yourself. You have to have purpose. Stay busy and have a purpose in life. My artwork gives me that purpose in life.

There was a time when being Indian or being Dakota brought about a feeling of not being proud for some, maybe even shame. I didn't feel that way. I always felt proud being Dakota, even though I had nothing to do with it. But we Dakota have some beautiful things that give us a positive attitude. Our art is making beauty, owaŋgwaśte wokaġa. Isn't that a good description—making something beautiful?

Stories Entertain

Stories provide a way to socialize and provide entertainment. Amusement and humor, reverence and awe, tragedy and fortune are ways to overcome wounded egos, blunders, boredom, and long winters.

The Tame Tataŋka

When I was a boy in the latter 1860s, our tribe was located in northwestern North Dakota after being driven out of our homes here by two military expeditions sent out by the government. We wanted to come back this way but were afraid other expeditions would be sent out against us and so were compelled to stay at a distance.

Up there, generally during the summer, our tribe split up, and all the more able-bodied ones with the best ponies went further northwest, sometimes to the Canadian boundary, while the old people and children and some of the women stayed in the location first mentioned. The reason the weaker ones did not follow so far northwest was because there was a good deal of danger up there from war parties of tribes located further away to the west.

The western section of the tribe got to the best buffalo range further away, and there was also more large game of all kinds up there further away, whereas we had to get along on small game, with now and then a buffalo or deer or elk. But there was a great plenty of fish in the streams where we were and also great amounts of all kinds of wild fruit.

Juneberries were very plentiful, and the women dried quantities of them. Also, there were strawberries. There seemed to be different varieties of these; some were of darker color than others, but all were of good size. Of course, there was no way of keeping these, and they could only be used fresh. These also grew much more luxuriant and bountiful in the tracks made by the travois where former tribes had traveled through years before.

The speaker in this story is not Grandpa Fred. He is retelling a story he heard from someone else long ago.

Of course, we didn't stay in one place all the time but always kept on the move. Although our day's marches were very short, as we didn't have good ponies to travel far or swift with, and we didn't need to, as we found plenty of whatever we needed in a small range.

Among the old people who knew the buffalo, there were always tales of mad or crazy buffaloes. It was always claimed that these were very dangerous, even with no provocation. And if one of these were wounded, it was the very limit of ferocity—charging a herd of ponies or a camp. They were odd in their habits, often not keeping with the herd but wandering alone.

One morning, as our camp was getting into the day's work, someone looking over the ponies tethered close to camp noticed a buffalo among the ponies. Immediately, everyone took up the cry: a crazy buffalo was coming near camp. Everyone was afraid, and most of us young ones climbed up in trees.

As there were no real able-bodied hunters in camp, it was considered too risky to try to kill the buffalo. But much to the people's surprise, instead of trying to do damage by attacking the ponies of the camp, the buffalo leisurely followed the trail back and finally went out of sight.

No one was expecting to ever see the mad buffalo again, and everyone was glad that it had left. That day, they made another short trip and camped again, and the buffalo was forgotten. But much to the people's surprise, the next morning, there he was among the ponies again. Of course, all were afraid of him and watched him closely, but he soon took the trail back again and went out of sight, thus relieving the worry at least for the time being.

That day, my brother-in-law, who is buried here, came back with one or two others, with a supply of dried meat for us from the buffalo-hunting camp. I don't know how they knew our whereabouts, but they found us anyway. The newcomers, upon hearing of the mad buffalo, said they would try to kill him in the morning, as he seemed bound to follow the camp and they expected he would be among the ponies the next morning.

So, that evening, all the ponies were tethered along the top of the bank of the stream just above the camp, and then the hunters in the morning could crawl up under cover of the bank and had no trouble getting within range and killing it.

The queer thing, though, was that the buffalo was not mad or crazy but was tame or at least partially tame. When they cut up the carcass, a rope was found tied around the neck, and a large-size sleigh bell was on the rope. This bell had a slot in it in the form of a cross, but one of the corners had been bent so that the piece of metal enclosed to make it jingle had fallen out.

They decided that this must have been one of the domesticated buffaloes that the Red River half-breeds had owned and which they used to haul their wooden carts with. This animal had probably wandered away and, the bell being damaged, they had no way of following it, so they left for another camping place. And the buffalo, being domesticated, had followed the first camp that he came to.

Close Encounters

My mother-in-law told me this story, that once while with her husband on a hunting trip, they camped out overnight in the Gros Ventre country. At that time, this tribe and the Sioux were enemies. Upon taking in their surroundings the next morning, her husband found the trail of a very large Gros Ventre war party that had passed a few rods from their camp. At another time, she and some other young women were picking cherries some distance from camp when she observed something pass through the tall grass. She hastily summoned her companions, and they got away just in time to escape another Gros Ventre war party. Upon reaching camp, she gave the alarm and the warriors sortied out, and a battle ensued in which a number on both sides were killed.

In earlier times, the Hidatsa people, a Siouan-speaking group, were known as the Gros Ventre of the Missouri. The Gros Ventre of the Prairie, later known as the Gros Ventre, are the A'aninin, an Algonquian-speaking group. Grandpa Fred is probably referring to the people now known as the Hidatsa.

Tawapahaȟota

The following story was told by Sampson James, whose tribal name was Tawapahaȟota. It illustrates how a young man used his wits to extricate himself from a certain position which he wished to get away from.

A young man of one of the Dakota bands had married a young woman of one of the neighboring villages. He lived there with his wife and father-in-law and two of his wife's sisters. Neither of the latter was married.

The young man himself was a very good hunter, so the household always had plenty of food. They got along nicely for some time, but the young man's wife died all of a sudden. After his wife's death, the young man thought of his own people and relatives and his own home. He decided to leave and go home to his own people. The old man felt very bad to lose him, as now they would have a hard time to get food.

The young man prepared a small pack of his possessions and bade them all goodbye and walked through the courtyard of the village and then out onto the prairie toward the home of his people. The old man sat in his lodge pondering their misfortune. Then he thought he saw a way by which he might be able to retain his son-in-law, and then they would always have plenty food.

Then he went outside the lodge and called to a young man passing by and said, "That young man leaving the village is my son-in-law. Go and call him back and tell him that I want to see him."

Not long after that, the son-in-law returned to the old man's lodge. He was sitting at the back of the lodge and welcomed the young man and asked him to sit down. He filled his pipe and lit it and passed it to his son-in-law and said that he wanted to talk to him about something very important.

The two girls were sitting to one side, possibly wondering what the old man had in mind. The younger of the two girls was nice-looking and had a clear complexion, but the other had rough skin.

The old man talked for some time about their past and always having plenty to eat, but if they were left to their own resources now, they would have a hard time, so he said he wished to keep the young man in the household. "On that account, I will let you marry either one of my daughters sitting here, and then you can stay with us and we will have plenty to eat."

The young man had his mind set on going home to his own people. He sat and smoked for some time, trying to think how to answer. He didn't want to actually refuse the old man's offer but was studying how to get out of this position gracefully, without causing too much hard feelings.

Finally, he said, "This young girl is nice-looking. If I should marry her, maybe some young fellow would take her away from me. So, in this case, I guess I will marry the other that is so rough-complexioned with scabs all over her face."

The girls listened to his talk and didn't like the slurs. One of them said, "That is too much. He says one of us would not be faithful to him and the other one of us he has to remark about the complexion. That is too much. Neither one of us is going to marry him." So saying, she arose and took her sister by the arm and led her outside the lodge.

The young man had achieved his end. He was now free to go home to his own people, and he had accomplished his end without actually refusing the old man's offer.

Learning Ojibwe

My mom's mother died when she was two years old, and subsequently Grandpa married Jane Brown, a Haȟatoŋwaŋ woman from White Earth who we called Grandma Jane. So, we were somewhat exposed to the Chippewa language and their long words, the classic being blueberry pie: miini-baashkiminasigani-biitoosijigani-bakwezhigan. So, we were not surprised when Grandpa had this sign, "Kwitcherbellyakin," on his wall and let us think that this was Chippewa. That is, until we tried to pronounce the word; then we all busted out laughing: "Grandpa, you were fooling us; that is not Chippewa."

*Fred Pearsall and
Jane Brown Pearsall,
Grandma Jane.*

The Cellar

Since Grandpa Waŋbdiska had no electricity and thus no refrigerator, he had an underground larder, or cellar, to store his food. Over this cellar he had a small building with a door that led in. Inside, over this opening, was this huge hide, perhaps a bear skin, to protect the inside temps from heat of summer and cold of winter. He told me, and I suspect other grandkids, to not go down there, as there were cici down there. In my next incarnation, when Grandpa tells me that, my response will be thus: "Grandpa, I am not motivated by fear; if you don't want me to go down there, just tell me, and I will obey. You don't have to use fear of mythical monsters to keep me out."

Reverend Tang

This story my tahaŋśi told about my parents, and it illustrates the use and uniqueness of idioms. An idiom is a grammatical term that expresses a thought that cannot be derived from a word-to-word translation.

There were church services at my parents' home one time (perhaps Lenten services), being led by our Presbyterian minister, who happened to be Chinese. Dad, being quite old at the time, excused himself to my mother in Dakota, saying that he was tired and going to bed. Sometime later, Reverend Tang noticed that Dad was gone and asked, "Where is Walter?" Mom replied, "He went to bed. He goes to bed with the chickens." If you were raised on a farm, you would understand the idiom: chickens go to the hen house early and roost—often before sunset. So Mom was saying that Dad always went to bed early. Reverend Tang understood it literally and was incredulous. He learned a new English saying that night.

Lonesome

After I graduated from Macalester College, I went to work for Burlington Northern Railroad, where I taught clerks a computer reporting system. Initially, it was kind of exciting working all over the system, though I was on the road (so to speak) for three weeks per month. This story took place in Quincy, Illinois, and West Quincy, Missouri. Somehow, I had become quite concerned with looks and clothes, as I always wore a suit or sport coat. In addition, I bought into the contact lens look. Back in the 1970s, they were quite large in comparison to today's lenses. Anyway, I worked the second shift at the depot and returned to the motel after midnight, when I decided to get a bite to eat before bed. When I entered the all-night diner, I sat down, and out of the corner of my eye, I spied another Indian. Oh, how unusual it seemed, way out of the way of any Indian reservation or concentration of Indians. I thought to myself, "Wow, there are no reservations near here. I bet he is as lonesome for Indians as me." Occasionally, I would look in his direction and he would be looking back. So I decided to go up and introduce myself. When I got up, I realized that I was looking into a full-length, full-width mirror. Damn contact lenses.

Exhibition Dancing

I have been dancing powwow for over three decades now. When I started, I lived in St. Paul, so I went to a certain number of Ḣaḣatoŋ-waŋ powwows, since they were fairly close. At that time, most of these powwows were not contests, and they sang almost exclusively their traditional songs with the fast beat. I was not used to their songs and did not know the song structure, so I did not know where I was in the song—kinda like when the southern drums started coming north. Anyway, I was at one of these powwows which had one Dakota drum, so I was waiting anxiously for their turn to sing. I danced some intertribal dances and then went outside the circle, not paying much attention to the emcee. Oliver Sudden I heard a good Dakota song. I cut my conversation short and ran out and danced. As I was dancing, I noticed that there were only little shavers dancing with me. I thought, oh, the adults probably don't like or don't know Dakota songs. Then I heard the emcee say something about a big Tiny Tot dancer. I figured who he was talking about but just kept on dancing and finished the song—a little embarrassed, but what the h . . . it was a good song. I was dancing an exhibition with the Tiny Tots.

Tataŋka Oyate

In the early '90s, I would go on a combination vacation and selling trip out west with my then wife, Dawn. She worked for the St. Paul schools, so we went during spring break, as I usually wasn't called back to construction work yet. So, it was an appropriate time for our trip. We were out to the Black Hills peddling my smoked deer and elk hides. We were traveling through Custer State Park at a pretty good clip, as the roads were empty, before tourist season. At one time I got an image of a buffalo and a notion of caution, so I slowed down, may have even braked. When we crested the hill, in the middle of the road was this huge buffalo, walking along. Dawn exclaimed, "Wow, we're lucky you slowed down. We surely would have hit that buffalo and probably been killed." No, it wasn't luck, nor coincidence. That experience has been my special connection to the Tataŋka Oyate—the Buffalo Nation.

Wamdoṡa

This was a story told by a community elder back in the day. As with many storytellers, she improvised and added in aspects to show her style.

Waziya (loosely translated as Old Man Winter, though literally it means North) just refused to leave—cold spell after cold spell, followed by snowstorm after snowstorm. Waziya was hanging on way too late; it must be March or even April. The Wamakaṡkaŋ Oyate (Animal People Nation) became worried and concerned, as they were afraid they were not going to survive. So they called a Tiyotipi to discuss and make plans. The consensus was that Wetu, Spring, had to be brought back north, and that would chase Waziya back to the North Pole. So they appointed Wamdoṡa (Redwing Blackbird) to fly south and bring Wetu back, as that was the fastest animal to accomplish this deed. So, Wamdoṡa did his job and flew down by Kansas City to bring back Wetu. So, in the spring, you will always see that the redwing blackbird is the first to come back, and we hear his call of "Okiŋni, okiŋni . . ." which means "Maybe, maybe spring is here." During this time, I will haul in one cart of wood a day—just enough for the day. I will be waiting for spring. Wetu, tokiya da he? Spring, where are you? Must we send Wamdoṡa to bring you north? "Okiŋni, okiŋni, okiŋni . . ."

To my way of thinking, Wamdoṡa sings "Okiŋni, okiŋni"— "Maybe, maybe"—because Wamdoṡa knows Waziya never leaves willingly. As he is retreating and melting, he will often throw us a six- to eight-inch snowstorm just to show us his power. And he leaves us with the warning that he will be back. This shows the tug to and fro of the seasons, maintaining equilibrium. Wamdoṡa, sometimes spelled amdoṡa, for the redwing blackbird: amdo means shoulder and ṡa means red.

The Host

Pejuhutazizi was like other communities and reservations where there were many good storytellers, so I will tell this one, though it is rather bare-boned. I heard this so long ago that I can only remember the gist of the story.

There was a Dakota traveler who had been walking for several days. He slept wherever he ended that day and foraged for whatever food nature provided. At the end of this day, he was hungry, thirsty, and exhausted when he came upon a rather unkept lone tipi—no others in sight.

Even as he approached the tipi, the voice of the owner greeted him with "Hau, hau, come on in and rest a bit." It was rather dark in there, so the traveler could not really see his host. But the host encouraged him to eat up, drink water, and rest. The traveler had not eaten so good for days and became sated and tired, so he told his host that he was going to lie down for a bit and sleep. "And I will see you in the morning."

In the morning, at the light of day, he awoke to see a skeleton, still clothed, in the back of the tipi. He became aware that his host was a ghost. He was, nonetheless, still grateful and went on his way. Mitakuye owasiŋ.

Bone Broth Soup

Bone broth soup reminds me of a Dakota family who were perhaps ahead of their time. Back in the late '50s or early '60s, there was a Dakota family from Pejuhutazizi who got their meat by visiting the dump grounds to find bones, meat, and fat from the carcasses of animals butchered and then discarded by the local meat market. They were there getting meat when they came across a human finger. "Oh my God—do we have an Ed Gein here in Minnesota?" they wondered. They notified the sheriff, and an investigation was started. They found out the butcher had cut off his finger with his band saw when cutting meat, and he threw it out with the carcasses. What does that say about America, when people have to get food from the dump?

The Crow

I don't know if this story is true, but it was told to me by my tahaŋśi, who was on a geological job looking for oil in the oil-shale belt. This was before the oil boom in North Dakota. He was working in Montana on the Fort Peck Reservation when they stopped in a bar. There were some Crows in there, possibly doing the same work, and they asked my tahaŋśi's group what kind of Indians they were. Tahaŋśi's group answered that they were Crow. The Crow guy thought for a minute and was doubtful that they were. So, he asked them to speak a little Crow to establish the truth. Of course, the Dakota boys had to come up with "Caw, caw . . ." That started the fight all over between the Crow and the Dakota.

The Rooster

When I was a toddler, perhaps three or four years old, our mean rooster chased me down our gravel driveway. When I fell, he pecked at my head. Dad, my hero, chased him around the yard until he caught him and killed him. We had him for supper. After that, I could not go in the chicken coop to pick eggs. If there were any in there, I sent in my tahaŋśi Lynn Blue, but by then we called him Punch, and he would go right in there among all the chickens to pick eggs. He even felt under sitting hens. He was younger than me, but to me he was brave. Later, I would not even consider going to Hitchcock's movie *The Birds*. I haven't been near a chicken coop since, so don't know if I would feel apprehensive today if I had to go in one. And, of course, we all know about the mean geese.

Synchronicity

A couple of years ago, Karen and I went to the Sioux Valley powwow in Manitoba. We were going through Virden when I noticed a Ford dealership and garage, but I didn't give much thought to it. The next day, a Saturday, I had trouble with my van; this was a holiday up there, too. I asked around about a garage that might be open and was directed to Brandon. But I remembered seeing the Ford garage in Virden, which was closer, and I knew where that was, instead of having to hunt through this larger town. So off we went to Virden, with the engine missing something terrible. As we pulled in, the mechanic there had already figured out that the spark plug blew out, taking the coil with it. But he was not working this Saturday. He said he just stopped in to wash his vehicle and he was headed home to take care of his son. And I would have to come back Tuesday when they reopened. I convinced him to fix my van on his day off, and I told him I would make it good for him. So, we went downtown to eat and came back a couple hours later, and it was done. I gave him a C-note for a tip and much thanks. Some would just say all these events were a coincidence, my noticing a Ford dealership and our arriving just as he was ready to leave. I give thanks for those. There were all kinds of other potential problems—not having the part, having to wait for parts.

Pandemic Travels

The tribe gave us elders frozen packaged American Airlines food during the pandemic. So, during my hibernation, I relived my traveling experience by carrying my suitcase on my treadmill for the length of an airport. Then I buckled myself into a chair with a tray, and Karen was the stewardess, bringing me my microwaved airline food. That is how I survived the hibernation and actually enjoyed my virtual trip to Europe.

Stories Tell of Place

We remember who we are and where we come from through stories of place. Land and place hold stories of origin, history, and knowledge and of our relationship with Ina Maka—Mother Earth.

The Eastern Dakota Bands

In the old times, there was a continuous string of Indian villages from the Lower Agency clear up to Browns Valley. There were some brush lodges stationed just above Browns Valley, where the elevator that the boat lands at is situated. At that time, there were a good many earth lodges located there.

The villages along the Minnesota River were established after the Treaty of 1851 required Dakota people to leave their traditional village sites in southern Minnesota and move to the reservation on the river.

The Chippeway were very troublesome at that time, too, and it was absolutely out of the question for a man to go off hunting alone. Even three or four were continually in danger, and to be safe there should be a party of twenty or so.

The earth lodges were made with centers dug out very deep, so that at the least sign of an attack of Chippeway, they immediately dropped down into the centers and were safe from any bullets that might be shot into the house promiscuously.

In the vicinity of the Lower Agency were located the seven villages of seven bands of Mdewakaŋtoŋwaŋ who had moved to that location from eastern Minnesota. Shakopee's band was up at Rice Creek. Little Crow's band was about three miles east of the town of Redwood Falls, Minnesota. Red Wing's band was located near the Lower Agency.

Then, at the Upper Agency were several bands of Waȟpetoŋwaŋ Dakota. Two or three miles west of the agency was the Hazelwood Republic, called the Log House Dwellers; in their own language, Caŋkaġotipi. This was close to the old missions of Riggs and Williamson. Up toward Montevideo was Red Iron's band.

Place Names

Bde Taŋka (Big Lake) = Lake Pepin

Ḣemnicaŋ (Still Water Wood. Probably refers to the wooded hill on the point in the river.) = Red Wing

Wakpa Taŋka (Big River) = Chippeway River, Wisconsin

Mini Sapa (Black Water) = Black River

Mini Sapa Ḣaȟa = Black River Falls

Iŋyaŋbasdata (Upright Stone) = Castle Rock

Grandpa Fred created this list of Dakota place names in 1912. His notes are now in the collections of the Minnesota Historical Society. Some of these names also appear in Stephen Riggs's dictionary.

Iŋyaŋbasdata Wakpa (Upright Stone River, named from Castle Rock) = Cannon River

Winona (First-born daughter. Beginning down the Mississippi River the town of Winona was named because one of Wapahaśa's daughters by that name, whom he loved greatly, was buried there. I don't know which Wapahaśa that was. The first daughter is called Winona. The modern pronunciation is Winuna.)

Wapahaśa (The town of Wabasha is named after the chief of that name, but the site also was called Mini Owe, which means spring or place to get water.)

Wazi Wita (Island of Pines. Pine Island was called Wazi Wita, both meaning the same.) = Pine Island

Owoboptedaŋ (Digging Place) = Appleton, and also Pomme de Terre River

Owoboptedaŋ (Digging Place. Digging place as in digging Indian turnips.) = Hastings

Cokaŋ Taŋka (Big Bottom Land Lake) = Newport

Iŋyaŋśayapi (Stone Painted Red. Refers to the Red Rock itself or, in fact, any worshipped and painted stone.)

Mdote or Bdote or Haḣabdote (Confluence or Confluence at the Falls) = Mendota

Wita Taŋka (Big Island. The island in the river at Mendota.) = Pike Island

Izuza Wita (Whetstone Island. A little rocky island in the bottom land lake across the river from Fort Snelling.)

Cokaŋ Haŋska (Long Bottom Land Lake. Across the Minnesota River from Fort Snelling.)

Icaḣtake (Touching Place. Where the river touches the bluff at Bloomington.) = Bloomington

Kaḣboke Ķtepi (Where the Drifter Was Killed. A little creek up the Mississippi River from Fort Snelling where a Sioux chief by that name was killed.)

Minihiŋḣpayedan (Little Water Fall. The modern Indian word for Miniḣaḣa Falls is Minihinḣpayedaŋ.)

Minii'ḣaḣa (Rapids. Accent on the third 'i.' Refers to any rapids.)

Ḣaḣa (Falls) = the falls at Minneapolis

Imnijaskadaŋ (White Cliff or Rock) = St. Paul

Ḣeyata Toŋwan Bde (Island Village Lake. Some people tried to imagine that it was called Mdoza or Mendoza Lake and the Minneapolis Park Board have tried to change the name to Lake Mendoza claiming it to be an Indian word whereas it is a Spanish name.) = Lake Calhoun

Heḣakahnakapi (Buried Elk) = Hamilton, now Savage

Tiŋtatoŋwaŋ (Prairie Town. Some of the early missionaries translated the name literally and called it Prairieville.) = Shakopee

Hdohdodowaŋpi (Growling Song) = Carver

Caŋhasaŋpaha (Hard Maple Hill) = Chanhassen

Makato Oze (Place to Get Blue Earth) = Blue Earth River

Maya Sapa (Black Cliff) = Mankato

Ḣeska (White Hill) = Henderson

Oiyuweġe (Crossing) = Traverse des Sioux or St. Peter

Waġaoju (Cottonwood Grove) = New Ulm

Ḣeyata Toŋwan Bde has had several Dakota names. Ḣeyata means "back by the hill, back from a river"; toŋwaŋ means village, and bde, lake. Because this name refers to a village, it may have been used after Maḣpiya Wicasta's village was established there in 1829. In 2018, the lake was renamed Bde Maka Ska.

The Riggs dictionary translates hodohdodowaŋ as "to sing a growling song. The Dakotas do so sometimes in going to war."

Riggs translates Isantanka, which means Long Knives, as "The name by which the Isaŋati Dakota designate the people of the United States. It is said to have been given them because the first Americans who came among the Dakotas were officers with swords."

Riggs translates iŋkpa as "at the end, at the head or source." This makes sense when referring to Big Stone Lake, the source of the Minnesota River.

Isaŋtaŋka Tipi (American's Home) = Fort Ridgely

Wapahaśa Wakpadaŋ (Wabasha Creek)

Iŋyaŋśa (Red Stone) = Pipestone

Caŋduhupaśa (Red Pipe. Both are used.) = Pipestone

Iŋkpa (End. Was the name of a chief who had a village at the south end of Big Stone Lake. It doesn't refer to Lac Qui Parle River. When the railroad was first built, that side was called Inkpa City but very soon was changed to Big Stone City.)

Ceġanawoju (Little Kettle Field. Someone by the name of Little Kettle planted there. Whetstone River, not Izuza [Grindstone].)

Wita Caŋṭe (Dead Wood Island) = Bird Island

Pteohaŋpi (Boiled Buffalo. Buffalo Lake which lies northeast of Montevideo and Granite Falls.) = Buffalo Lake

Wakpaipakśaŋ (Crooked River. This name refers particularly to the stretch near Flandreau.) = Sioux River

Maya Wakaŋ (Holy Bank) = Chippeway River, the one at Montevideo. Probably called Chippeway River because the Chippeways more in the habit of descending it on war parties. Some say that Maya Wakaŋ was a name given by former tribe.

Bde Caŋ (Wood Lake) = Battle Lake

Hiŋtawoju or Hintahaŋkpanwoju (Planting Place of Basswood Moccasin Strings) = Wood Lake

Mini Taŋka (Big Water) = Niobrara River and town in Nebraska

Ptaŋsiŋte (Otter Tail) = Browns Valley

Wakiŋaŋoye or Wakiŋyaŋ Oye Bde (Thunder Track or Thunder Track Lake) = Some small lakes west of Lake Traverse. Nicollet's translation is correct.

Bde Witatowa (Lake with Islands) = Marsh Lake south of Appleton

Know Your People

Back in the early '70s, maybe late '60s, when they rerouted Highway 23, the construction uncovered a Ṡahiyena (Cheyenne) camp. Somehow the archeologists who studied the site could determine it was Ṡahiyena rather than Dakota. But that made sense, in that the Cheyenne were the first ones to follow the Minnesota River out of the Minnesota woodlands to the prairie west, followed by the Lakota. Good thoughts to the Ṡahiyena runners.

I want to determine what kind of Indian I am. I don't want Lakota or waṡicuŋ to tell me what kind of Dakota I am. I am a Sisitoŋwaŋ Waȟpetoŋwaŋ Dakota. I am not Isaŋati (Santee)! Those people live in Nebraska, Flandreau, Lower Sioux, Ṡakpe, and Prairie Island. We Sisitoŋwaŋ Waȟpetoŋwaŋ, of course, live here at Pejuhutazizi, at Sisseton, and at Spirit Lake, and I suspect at Standing Buffalo in Canada, as he was a Sisitoŋwaŋ Waȟpetoŋwaŋ chief. This is the reason I tell my grandchildren which band they are from, not just Upper Sioux.

Maya Bdeġa

Back in the '50s, Dad told me about Maya Bdeġa, or Pelican Hill. This is some place on Bdehdakiŋyaŋ, or Lake Traverse, I think on the east side of the lake. There was a camp or village of Dakota on a hill above Lake Traverse. It was buffalo-hunting time, so all the men except the elderly were out hunting the buffalo. So there were just women, children, and the elderly in camp when somebody spotted a Ȟaȟatoŋwaŋ (Chippewa) war party coming down the lake in canoes. Of course,

Dekśi Super's pelican drum.

this caused all kinds of worry and consternation, as they did not know how to protect themselves when all the men were out hunting. A peculiar thing about this camp was that they had a pelican trained as a pet. Somebody remembered the pelican, so they put it in the tipi with a war bonnet on it and lit a fire so that its silhouette was visible from outside. The rest of the camp fled to a wooded coulee and hid. Sure enough, the Ḣaḣatoŋwaŋ attacked, and seeing the tipi with a chief in it, they attacked that first. They went in and saw the pelican. Thinking that those Dakota have bigger medicine because their chief turned himself into a pelican, they fled. The pelican saved their lives, and so this hill was called Pelican Hill.

This story, "Maya Bdeġa," was produced in an animated short by Pioneer Public TV and won awards. I am sure Dad would be astounded about this recognition, and I am also sure his mother would be, as that is who told him the story of Maya Bdeġa. See, Dad—I was listening.

Owobopte Wakpa

Another of Mother's ancestors was Tacaŋhpi Kokipapi, translated as They Are Afraid of His War Club. He earned this name in the fight with the Ḣaḣatoŋwaŋ at Owobopte Wakpa—the Place Where the Dakota Turnips Have Been Dug River, or Pomme de Terre River—near Appleton, Minnesota.

> The battle on the Owobopte Wakpa took place in 1818. An Ojibwe leader of the Pillager band named Black Dog led a party of sixteen Ojibwe men into Dakota country. They were discovered by a large party of Dakota who were camped at this river. The Dakota killed all but one Ojibwe; thirty-three Dakota were killed.

Rice Creek

Upriver a little ways from Cedar Rock, in Redwood County, is a creek called Rice Creek, emptying into the Minnesota from the south. Grandpa told me at one time we Dakota used to harvest psiŋ, wild rice, from that creek—thus its name.

Caŋśaśa Wakpadaŋ

On my walk, I pass a creek we call Waŋyeca Wakpadaŋ—in English, Firefly Creek. The waśicuŋ call this Hazel Creek. Joseph Nicollet made a trip up the Minnesota River with Dakota guides, recording place names and mapping the area, back in the 1830s. His journal has been published, and he places the name of Caŋśaśa Wakpadaŋ on our creek. In English, it would be called Red Willow Creek. And that name seems so apt, as when I was a preteen, my brother Gordy and

> Joseph Nicollet, a French geographer and astronomer, mapped the Mississippi and Missouri basins. His journal has been published as *Joseph N. Nicollet on the Plains and Prairies* (St. Paul: MNHS Press, 1976).

I went gathering caŋśaśa, using Grandpa's instructions and directions, for tobacco. Caŋśaśa is red willow tobacco used for smoking—Indian tobacco, perhaps. Today, mainly red osier dogwood is being used, and the preparation I see the young do now is way different than the method we used. So I think both types have been used.

We used what we called red willow. It used to grow right here on our creek, but I don't see it anymore. It grew alongside the green willow, that willow used for making initipi, sweat lodges, and it had a reddish color but was not as red as the dogwood. We waited until "after the thunder beings came" and the willow was sucking up moisture. We cut the plant so that it could regrow next year, and with the moisture, the two barks—the outer and the inner—could be separated easily from the stem wood and each other. These inner bark strippings were hung to dry. Later, it was crumpled up when dry and cut with regular tobacco if so desired; then it could be smoked. It has a most beautiful and pleasant smell, which is absent from the dogwood. Grandpa often smoked his pipe in the evening for pleasure—no ceremonial purpose then. A couple of years ago, I was at Big Bend powwow on the Crow Creek Reservation, and their arbor was covered in willow, and lo and behold I saw the red willow. I recognized it immediately. Of course, nobody else knew what I was talking about.

Upper Sioux Agency

Some thirty to forty years ago, when I read Gabriel Renville's Narrative at the Minnesota Historical Society, I shared, like others, the wonder and awe of holding a historic piece of paper—one that Tiwakaŋ held in his hands. After Gabriel's death, his son Victor gave this manuscript to Sam Brown, Gabriel's nephew, and the historical society published an English translation made by Brown and Thomas

Samuel Brown was the son of Joseph R. Brown, a fur trader, politician, and Indian agent, and Susan Frenier Brown, a French-Dakota woman; Samuel had served as a scout for Sibley's forces after 1862. Thomas Robertson was the son of trader Andrew Robertson and Jane Anderson Robertson, a British-Dakota woman; he became a translator and fought with Little Crow's forces in order to protect his family.

Robertson, from H̓eipa. When I read that, I calculated that Tiwakaŋ lived about five miles north of Upper Sioux Agency, which happens to be pretty close to where I now live. He continues by telling about crossing the river and riding up out of the valley to the prairie atop. I know most of the river from the confluence of the Yellow Medicine to Granite Falls, and I believe there is only one spot along there where there is a ford in the river, and that happens to be right below my place. So, I think he rode by where my house stands today. At that spot, our creek flows into the river with a sandbar, thus lowering the water with no steep banks.

I was curious as what word Tiwakaŋ used for miles, so I went to the Minnesota Historical Society to see the original Dakota. Was it caŋkuoiyute—road measure? I made copies of both the original Dakota written and the translated one. Tiwakaŋ used the term makaiyutapi—quite a clever word. Maka means earth, and iyutapi means measure, so "earth measure" for mile. Today a Dakota speaker would more than likely just use the English word, mile.

H̓eku and Kaȟmiŋ

H̓eku and Kaȟmiŋ are two village sites here, used long before our reservation was established. H̓eku means below the hill in Dakota. Bob St. Claire and his family came to integrate our little village. See, we were ahead of our time in integration, since he is H̓ahatoŋwaŋ and a relative of mine. The Starlights and Maude Ortley lived below the hill, back off the highway, perhaps a mile or so. That was kind of near where Pejuhutazizi Church use to be, but of course that was before my time—my older sisters remember when it was there. The Marlowes lived by the river. Rufus and Verna Ross lived here, too, before they moved to the other village, Kaȟmiŋ, which was upriver a couple of miles. One of the names at Kaȟmiŋ was an Ironheart family, but Fred Blue did not think they were related to Herbert Ironheart's family, as they did not show a kinship relationship. And that brought to mind a Rev. Solomon Tuŋkaŋsaiciye (tuŋkaŋ can mean a big boulder or father-in-law; saiciye means paints himself red), who is buried in our cemetery. In one book I read that he ministered to his relatives at Moose Mountain Dakota Reserve in Canada—now called Whitecap Reserve—shortly after 1862. I believe he comes from this other

Ironheart family. I would like to go to this Whitecap Reserve to find out if anyone remembers hearing about this Reverend Tuŋkaŋsaiciye.

Iyakaptapi—refers to the Ascension Church near Big Coulee, South Dakota, and loosely translates as They Go Up, or They Ascend—got me thinking about my mother's family history. My mother's mother, Wakaŋtiomaniwiŋ (Spirit Walking in the House), was baptized, and I assume born, at Makaġiiyuzapi—the Brown Earth Settlement near Milbank, South Dakota, as noted in the *Iapi Oaye*, the newspaper of the Presbyterian Church. Her parents were Hotoŋtoŋna (Animal Makes a Noise) and Taśinasusbecawiŋ (Her Dragonfly Blanket Woman). Hotoŋtoŋna's father was Owakeyaduta (Red Lodge). After the influence of the missionaries, I suspect he took on the name of Amos Owakeyaduta. Hotoŋtoŋna followed in somewhat the same fashion and took the first name of Joseph, and he is referred to as Joseph Hotoŋtoŋna in the paper trail. Later on, he changed his last name to reflect his father's name somewhat and took the last name of Amos. Thus, his gravestone here at our cemetery says Joseph Amos. Hotoŋtoŋna developed tuberculosis and wanted to die in Minnesota, so they moved to the Pejuhutazizi area but lived up the road a couple of miles from here at Ḣeku, Below the Hill Village. He died in the 1890s.

That was a place where several members of a family lived at different times, the last being Pansy and Bud St. Clair—a family not related to Bob. Of course, my grandpa Waŋbdiska lived here, and across the road from him lived Annie Adams. Now, Ḣeku is just a memory. It is all gone; no one lives there. I am sure there are young people who drive by and never give it a thought or know. Life moves on, never stays the same. There were other Dakota who lived here before me, and others will follow.

Pejuhutazizi

I have always felt rather isolated here at Pejuhutazizi from other Dakota, Nakota, and Lakota people because of the separation for generations. So, it always amazes me when we all share certain cultural peculiarities which I thought were only practiced here. Yet I hear others talk of cici man, and having children bend over and look through their legs to see their next sibling. Perhaps there are more which we have in common.

• • • •

In the fall, the men of Pejuhutazizi would spend a day cutting wood and hauling it into the basement of the community hall so we would have fuel for winter doings. It is hard to imagine that happening today—getting together and working for a common good. Whenever we had big chunks of wood that we could not burn at home, we hauled them down to the hall, as the hall furnace could take huge pieces of wood.

In my youth, whether it was in homes or the community hall, we played cards—not the gambling kind. The women played Flinch and the men played whist or sometimes hearts. Oh, man! I haven't played cards for years. On New Year's Eve, we started the wood furnace in the community hall early so it would be nice and warm by evening. And everybody brought food, and the adults played cards. And at midnight, the old (man) year was chased out by the new (baby) year. The rest of the Christmas apples and candy bags were passed out to all. This was before drinking to celebrate the new year took over. One year, we had powwow—that was the year my sister Deb was born; her Indian name is Omaka Teca Wiŋ.

• • • •

Back in the heyday of relocation—'50s and early '60s—when reservation Indians went off to the big cities to make a new life with the encouragement of the government, a good share of them returned to the reservation from Los Angeles, Chicago, Cleveland, etc. I would often hear the adults say that if the government relocated Indians to the moon, somehow they would find their way home. That sentiment of wanting to go home seemed to be especially strong with us Dakota. On the metaphorical side, I saw it with Dad when he was in his eighties or nineties. He said that he awoke every morning with a prayer of gratitude for living another day but that he was ready anytime now, Wakaŋtaŋka, to go home and see his mother and other family members. Now those two views—gratitude for life and an acceptance of leaving—are not diametrically opposed or incongruent. I understand what Dad meant, and it was no way a wish to die but an acceptance that there was a time to move on home.

Stories Provide Belonging

When you know your story, no matter where you go, you belong. Stories have roots to the past that lead all the way back to the source of all things. Stories connect the past to the present, thus shape future realities. Stories are a bridge between generations past and grandchildren yet to come. Dakota stories remind us to think about the consequences of our actions seven generations forward, reflecting upon the legacy of seven generations before. Stories bring us home.

Wopida Cerisse for sharing the stories from Grandpa Fred—our family's legacy—and making sure we would not forget who we are.

Susbe

Your grandmother, Tašinasusbecawiŋ, was from the old Mdewakaŋtoŋwaŋ band of eastern Minnesota. She was from the Wapahaśa village
of that band and was born at Pine Island in eastern Minnesota and was
always told that she was one of a pair of twins but the other died when
very young.

Your grandmother said that her grandparents, probably on her mother's side, were from the Waḣpekute band of the eastern Dakota people
who inhabited southeastern Minnesota. The old man's name was
Wayahuġa, which means Cruncher, and the lady's name was Wiŋpteca,
which means Short Woman.

Her father was one of seven brothers. I heard the name of only one,
that was Ceġa-apa. Up along the Flint River of Wisconsin, which flows
into the Mississippi, there was a cave in the bank, which was supposed
to be inhabited by some kind of spirits or supernatural beings. Her
father and his brothers had a habit of going to this cave, and they had
encounters with these spirits and received visions from them. Such visions as they may have received in such places as this would sometimes
affect a man's whole life.

After the treaty of 1851, your grandmother with her family and of course
the rest of the band moved into the western part of Minnesota along the
river near where Rice Creek joins the Minnesota River. They made a village there and lived there contentedly for a few years. This creek received
its name because some wild rice grows beside it near its mouth.

As a girl, she moved with her family to western Minnesota and after
1862 wandered all over North Dakota and Manitoba. After she was
married in Canada, she and her husband returned to the United States
and took a homestead at Flandreau, South Dakota.

Refugees

After they left Minnesota in 1862, they traveled slowly and hunted between times and got out to the Missouri River. The next winter, they
camped at the forks of the Little Missouri. That winter, there was a
very large camp there. There were several different bands, each camping by themselves and forming several different villages, each separate
from the other but all close together.

The Métis hunted all through this region, traveling as entire villages, in the same way that the Dakota themselves traveled when hunting buffalo. This camp was not a permanent village site, but just one of many temporary campsites.

The hub of the camp was a party of Red River half-breeds, some of whom were traders. They had several log houses where they lived and carried on their trade with the Indians. This half-breed village was afterward broken up by the military and all the buildings burned, as they got to selling too much strong liquor to the Indians. Which caused a good deal of trouble.

• • • •

In 1862, my maternal great-grandmother, Taśinasusbecawiŋ—a member of Wapahaśa's band, which lived a few miles east of the Lower Agency—and her family were digging pipestone at the quarry. When they were returning home, they found out about the start of the war. Of all the horror stories from 1862 that my family has told me about, the most emotional for me is the story of my mother's family. I get choked up telling it, even though they fled before the war was over and thus did not experience Fort Snelling and the expulsion from Minnesota. They fled north and west.

The family spent one year hunting buffalo with the Red River Métis all over what would become North Dakota and Montana before finding refuge in Canada. These Métis were of Ojibwe and European (mostly French) ancestry, and they developed their own culture. They were known for the Red River oxcarts delivering buffalo hides to St. Paul. Some of these Métis later became members of Ojibwe reservations, namely Turtle Mountain.

My great-grandmother's family finally ended up in Canada as refugees. She did not come back until the 1880s or '90s. They became refugees and had to leave home because of war, much as today's refugees have fled, and now they are treated with disdain instead of compassion. Was my grandmother treated that way?

• • • •

Those Red River people were very much attached to dancing, and quite a number of them were good violinists. Grandma sometimes attended those dances, and a young man of half-breed took quite a liking to her. She didn't know but that he might have wanted to marry her, but nothing happened, and the next season they went to Canada, as they knew that a great many of their own tribal members had gone there already, and they had many old friends and neighbors and relatives there.

They wandered over Canada for several years, and during that time they had contact with other tribes and the Red River half-breeds, which were really a tribe by themselves and were considered as such by the other Indians, as they had their own customs and language—the latter being a mixture of French, Chippeway, and some other Indian languages.

These old people were great talkers, and they had good memories and were always telling old-time tales about their ancestors.

While they were in Canada, she became friendly with a young man, and after some time, they expected to get married. He had given her a finger ring and they were expecting to mate up soon. But the young man went on a warpath against the Chippeway and was killed, so that ended that romance.

While up there, they got used to using black tea and liked it very much. Afterward, when they came home here, they always remembered it, but it was seldom that it could be found in the stores here. If some store here happened to have some, it was a big piece of news among the neighbors, and they all wanted to get some.

She seems to have been alone with her father up there, but he must have died up there. Anyways, sometime later, she married a young man up there by the name of Maḣpiya Waṡtedaŋ.

At one time when they were up there, they camped on the shore of a large lake one winter. There must have been a Hudson's Bay Company post there, as there was a post office of a kind that the mail carriers brought mail to. She said the lake was so large that they could see the mail carrier with his dog team coming across the lake for two days before he reached the trading post and post office.

The Hudson's Bay Company, a British firm, began trading for furs on Hudson Bay in 1670 and for many years dominated the Canadian trade. By the 1860s, it had lost its monopoly and was establishing stores in Canada's new population centers. It continues to operate in Canada.

All those that were across the border got acquainted with the fine wool blankets that were put out by the Hudson's Bay Company and they always liked them, and after they returned here, they always remembered them and wanted to get one if possible. If they saw one of those blankets, they recognized it immediately.

• • • •

Here is another one of the stories my great-grandmother Taśinasusbecawiŋ told Grandpa. She and her family escaped to Canada after 1862, and they lived on this big lake; I wonder which one it was. Grandma said that mail was brought by dogsled and the person bringing it came across this lake and they could see him coming for two or three days before he came to their village. It also seems that there were existing Dakota here in Canada, as that is where they sought refuge—with other Dakota.

Taśinasusbecawiŋ was about twelve years old in 1862, and so she spent a good share of her life up in Canada. She was going to marry this Dakota by the name of Śiowicaśta (Prairie Chicken Man). He was killed out hunting or on war raid; I can't remember which. She must have been quite distraught, and she decided to come back to this side of the border. She eventually married Hotoŋtoŋna (Animal Makes a Noise). He eventually took the English name of Joseph Amos and was, of course, from Iyakaptapi at Sisseton. So, if circumstance were different, she probably would have stayed in Canada—and Me? There would be no Me.

The Return

Sometime later, they decided to return to the United States. Some others who were associated with them wanted to return, too.

A great many of the people that went to Canada never wanted to return here, as they had received such unfair and dishonest treatment from the crooked officials here that they wanted to stay away if possible. Others had the homing instinct too strong and decided to come back to their own country, even in the face of obstacles. Many were afraid to come back, as they would be accused of starting the outbreaks of 1862, when it was the traders who had started all the trouble.

At any rate, along about 1867, it seems that your grandmother and several others decided to come back home. She must have been about seventeen or eighteen years of age then.

Well, how do you think they traveled in those days? They didn't go by airplane, nor railroad, nor bus. They had no wagons and buggies, and if they did have, there was no place where they could get repairs if they had a breakdown.

Their only vehicle was the tent poles tied over the horse's back and dragging behind. Back of the horse a frame is tied on the poles, and a load of blankets, kettles, tent cover, etc. was tied on this. The people walked, and some that had them rode horseback. They did not travel very far in a day when a village was moving, but young men on foot alone were very swift, and for one to travel fifty miles in a day was very common.

On their way at this time, coming back to the Missouri River, they came one afternoon or evening to what they thought was a good camping place. Upon starting to put up their tents, they began examining the surroundings and saw several dead buffaloes lying around where they were going to camp, near the water. They suspected that the water was poison from some natural cause and had killed the buffalo, and so they were afraid to use any of it. They had to stick it out that night without any water, as it was too late to hunt up another camping place that evening.

Sometime after this, they arrived at the Missouri River, and there the party seems to have broken up and your grandmother was alone with her husband. Once, they were traveling alone not far from the river in a rolling or hilly country. The man had shot a deer that day, and they were depending on the meat during their trip, so at evening time they found a nice camping place among the hills. They gathered dry wood and they cut up the deer, and all the heavy meat of it they sliced it for drying.

Then they built a frame up off the ground and made a fire under it and spread the sliced meat on the frame and dried it in the heat of the fire and smoke. Late in the evening, after dark, they were done. She was expecting they would sleep right there near the fire and the meat drying. This was warm weather, and they traveled light and made no tent. She was preparing a bed near the fire and meat drying, but the man said they must not do that, as war parties were out all the time, and if they slept there, they might be found and killed.

So, he led her up a ravine and around the back of a rise of ground about a quarter of a mile from the campfire. Here they bedded down for the night. Early in the morning, he got up and said he must go and look at the ponies. After a little while he returned, and Grandma saw by the expression on his face that something terrible must have happened. She asked him what was the matter. He said, "We are lucky. We just saved ourselves. A big war party of Ree passed by here not very long ago, and we were lucky that we hid in this ravine for the night."

How he knew what tribe that war party was from is not plain, but that was common in the west. If anyone came upon the trail of a different tribe, they always were able to tell what tribe had made the trail.

Flandreau Settlement

Neither one of them could read or write, and so there was no chance of their receiving any mail, but just as at present time, the grapevine was a very persistent carrier of news. From that source they knew about the settlement of the Mdewakaŋtoŋwaŋ, or Santee, at Flandreau, South Dakota, which started in 1869. That settlement or community was several dozen families that left the reservation at Santee, Nebraska, and came up to Flandreau and took homesteads on government land, the same as the white men did.

For a few years, they got along fairly well, as there was quite a bit of good hunting yet, and they made most of their living in that way. But when their natural way of living began to give out, they got into hard times. Then they began to lose their lands, as they began to go in debt

The Flandreau Colony was started in 1869 by twenty-five families that left the Santee Reservation in Nebraska without authorization, while the agent was away in Washington. They gave up tribal rights and annuities in order to take up farms and be free of both government agents and tribal leaders. After years of great difficulty, and with some government assistance, the colony succeeded; it became a reservation in 1936 under the Indian Reorganization Act.

and mortgage their homesteads. Some went to Nebraska, but most of them stayed and made out to exist on small pieces of land.

Those Flandreau people were Grandma's own tribe, and she was related to or acquainted with most of them. So, they decided to come to Flandreau and make a home among their own people. They made the trip across the country and arrived at the Flandreau settlement. Like the other Indians there, they took a homestead of government land and built a log house on it and did their best to farm, although they did not know much about tilling the soil. But, like the others there, hunting and trapping was an important part of their living.

Visiting Family

Your grandmother had a sister or first cousin living at Wabasha, Minnesota. She wished to see her and her family. This sister was married to a French man named Trudell, and he had quite a large family, all boys. By this time, Grandma had a son of her own, and with him she made the trip to Wabasha, Minnesota. She must have been with someone else, as she would not be very likely to make a trip alone, and there were no railroads at that time that she could go on. The only traveling at that time was on foot, or horseback, or wagon and team, if anyone had such a vehicle.

When she got to Wabasha, she found her sister and also some other of her relatives. Her sister's children were pretty well grown up by that time. The man being French, he necessarily was Catholic, as were his family, and on that account they prevailed upon her to join them, and they had her baptized and a name was given her according to the church and the white people's custom, but she never knew the name or else could not pronounce it, so she forgot it promptly. Her husband, Maȟpiya Waṡtedaŋ, did not go with her on this trip. It must have been that he was afraid of the white people and did not dare to go among them.

Therefore, during the time that she was making the trip to Wabasha, her husband made a trip up to the Hill Head country at Sisseton, and she said he stayed near Buffalo Lake. Probably he had some relative living there. While he was staying there, he suddenly had taken sick and died and was buried there.

Starting Over

She returned to Flandreau to her home and had the little boy with her. Your grandfather lived close to her, but at that time he was married to another woman by the name of Tipiojaŋjaŋwiŋ. They had some children, but all died very young, according to the general run of the Indians at that time. The whites had forced them into poor living conditions, vegetable food, and poor ventilation of their dwelling places, also thick clothing that kept the healthy suntan off the skin. This all worked to undermine their health, so nearly all went into tuberculosis and died young. Of course, the white people were glad of that, as they wished to see them exterminated.

In those days, the birth of a child in a family was often an occasion of sorrow rather than happiness. They would say that child will not live very long. What is the use of that child coming on the earth only to die soon and leave us to mourn for him?

After your grandfather got his divorce from his first wife, he was free to marry again. He, with your grandmother, left Flandreau and came up to the Brown Earth Settlement near Milbank, South Dakota. I do not know what became of the homestead that was your grandmother's. Brown Earth was north of the town of Flandreau, several miles from town along the river. The Indians there all took land along the river so that they had wood to burn and also for building log houses. When the white farmers came, they also sold wood to them, too.

Hotoŋtoŋna

As for your grandfather, he died before I was married to your mother, and so I never heard anything from him in regard to his life. His name was Hotoŋtoŋna, and his father's name was Owakeyaduta. I never saw either one of them. Your grandfather died here at Granite Falls, Minnesota, in the spring of 1899.

I never knew which village of the Waḣpetoŋwaŋ Dakota your grandfather belonged to. There were seven different bands or villages of the Waḣpetoŋwaŋ scattered through southern Minnesota. The village farthest east was the Wiyaka Otidaŋ up the river a short distance above Shakopee. He might have been from that band, as he associated with the Mdewakaŋtoŋwaŋ a good deal, and they were the ones that lived from Shakopee down the river.

But of course, after the Treaty of 1851, they were all gathered along the Minnesota River on what they had reserved as a home for the tribe up in this part of the country.

Hotoŋtoŋna's mother's name was Kata, and she was claimed to be from the Sac and Fox tribe, those who are now located in Iowa near Tama and Toledo. She used to speak the Sac and Fox language, and from association with her, your mother learned a few words and expressions from that language. I have heard her sometime use strange words, and she said, "Grandma taught me those words out of the Sac and Fox language." Your great-grandmother Kata died at Flandreau, South Dakota, during the 1890s. Your great-grandfather died a few years later, but I do not know where.

Kata and Owakeyaduta had seven children, but only two survived, one being Hotoŋtoŋna. Owakeyaduta translates as Red Lodge. He later takes the name Amos Owakeyaduta.

Owakeyaduta was one of the old-time people and had been on the

The Sac and Fox people (Sauk and Meskwaki) lived south of the Dakota in what is now southern Minnesota and Iowa. The Waḣpetoŋwaŋ had frequent interaction with them; the Dakota were said to be allies of the Sac and Fox.

warpath several times. We used to have an old tomahawk head made of steel or iron which he had used when he was on the warpath. That tomahawk head is now in the museum of the Yellow Medicine County Historical Society. The old man valued it very highly, as he used to tell of the time he killed a Chippeway with it up in the vicinity of Appleton, Minnesota. The Chippeway were constantly sending war parties down south here to raid the Dakota villages along the Minnesota River.

The missionaries had at some time got some influence over Owakeyaduta and must have baptized him and gave him the name Amos. So your grandfather took the name as a last name, and he was Joseph Amos. And his brother, who you girls knew up in the Iyakaptapi or Ascension region, was David Amos.

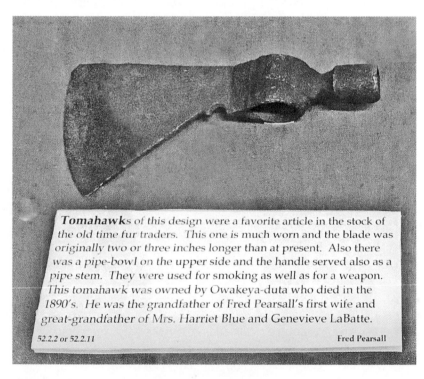

Tomahawks of this design were a favorite article in the stock of the old time fur traders. This one is much worn and the blade was originally two or three inches longer than at present. Also there was a pipe-bowl on the upper side and the handle served also as a pipe stem. They were used for smoking as well as for a weapon. This tomahawk was owned by Owakeya-duta who died in the 1890's. He was the grandfather of Fred Pearsall's first wife and great-grandfather of Mrs. Harriet Blue and Genevieve LaBatte.

52.2.2 or 52.2.11   Fred Pearsall

Owakeyaduta's tomahawk head. Courtesy Yellow Medicine County Historical Society

Brown Earth, Sisseton

In the Brown Earth community, Rev. Daniel Renville was the minister, and he performed the marriage ceremony for them. They lived there several years, and during that time, your mother was born. The little boy was now grown up, and while they lived at Brown Earth, he married a woman from the Sisseton Reservation by the name of Inajin Win. That woman was a half sister to Charley Quinn's father.

About this time, the government was getting ready to take the Sisseton Reservation away from the Indians, on account of the Brown Earth Settlement breaking up, and all the members went up to the reservation.

There, they all took allotments out of the tribal land. Your grandmother had an allotment of 160 acres, your grandfather had an allotment of 160 acres, your mother had an allotment of 160 acres, an aunt of yours had an allotment of 160 acres (her name was Agnes, but she

The Brown Earth community was started in 1875, when about twenty-five families left the Sisseton Reservation and traveled about forty miles to the southwest to begin farming, evidently because of factional disputes and a change in the Indian agent. They built the Brown Earth Church, which still stands, in 1877. Although they managed to get some agricultural supplies from the agent at Sisseton, the colony was not successful. Most people moved back to Sisseton in the late 1880s, when the reservation was allotted; historian Roy Meyer writes that "a few wanted nothing to do with reservations, and migrated to Minnesota, where they formed the nucleus of the present Upper Sioux Community near Granite Falls."

Under the Dawes Act of 1887, the federal government began forcing Native American tribes to subdivide their reservations and allot separate parcels to individual tribal members. Unallotted lands were then sold to white settlers, with the income supposedly being invested in programs to benefit the tribes. The effects of this policy were disastrous. Tribal land bases were lost; landholdings became fractionalized; many individuals lost their land for nonpayment of taxes. Ninety million acres—about two-thirds of the tribal lands in the United States—were lost between 1887 and 1934.

died very young), and an uncle of yours had an allotment of 40 acres. This last boy was entitled to 160 acres, but your grandparents said, "He will never live to make use of it, so what is the use of taking any more land for?" So, no more land was allotted to him.

They lived on their allotments for a few years, but your grandfather was not in very good health, so he wanted to come back to Minnesota, his old home, where the climate was not so rough.

Coming Home

They broke up their home near Ascension where their land was located and came to Granite Falls, Minnesota, in 1897. They stayed here with some of their relatives. It was Pazi and his wife, Itate, that they stayed with, as they had no home of their own here. Those are the grandparents of Emma Jackson, and Pazi was the father of Andrew Hepaŋna, you girls all remember him. By this time, your grandfather was well advanced in TB, and he knew that he would not live very long.

Then they went back to their old home on their allotments and stayed a few months, and in 1898, they came again to Granite Falls, Minnesota. There they bought a small piece of land and built a small house. Not long afterward, they traded that small piece of land for the piece where our house is now located, and they had the house moved onto this last piece that they had traded for.

By the time they had got to living in this present location, your grandfather was getting quite low with TB. He stayed outdoors in the fresh air as much as possible and in a tent part of the time. He used to lay on a blanket outside the house and pull up the grass and weeds and make a bare spot beside the house. Among the grass and weeds a little box elder tree had started, maybe five or six inches high. This he left and said that he would let that tree grow.

Adam and Nancy (Itate or Wind Woman) Pazi were married on April 13, 1876. They were also a part of the Brown Earth community before returning to Pejuhutazizi.

Your grandmother kept that tree, and it grew up to be that tree that stood close to the house on the east side. But a few years ago, it had got so that it shaded the house too much, which caused the shingles to rot. Also, the squirrels used to climb it and get into the house, and they even ate holes in the roof, so a few years ago I cut it down just to save the house.

Your grandfather died in the spring of 1899 here and was buried up in the cemetery on the hill here.

Hotoŋtoŋna's Death

Sometime after my great-grandmother Tašinasusbecawiŋ returned from Canada, she married Hotoŋtoŋna, a Wahpetoŋwaŋ who had previously married an Isaŋati woman who came from the Flandreau area from the Eastman family. After his divorce, Hotoŋtoŋna and Susbe moved to the Iyakaptapi area of the Sisseton Reservation. They became dissatisfied with the reservation life and moved to the Brown Earth Settlement, called Makaġiiyuzapi. They were following the example of the Isaŋati people leaving the Santee Reservation in Nebraska for land near what would become Flandreau. In their case, they got government help to settle, but not from Sisseton; the agent said if you are leaving the reservation, you cannot take plows, horses, etc. So they endured on their own without government help. This lasted a number of years, but eventually the settlement failed, and they returned to the Sisseton Reservation. Hotoŋtoŋna eventually got tuberculosis and wanted to die in his previous home in Minnesota, so they moved to the Granite Falls area. He died here in the 1890s and is buried in our cemetery. Hotoŋtoŋna eventually took the English name of Joseph Amos, taking the last name of Amos, which his father took as a first name and became known as Amos Owakeyaduta and later just Amos Red Lodge.

After the death of Hotoŋtoŋna, Tašinasusbecawiŋ married Mazaowaŋca (Iron All Over), a Presbyterian minister, and he is also buried in our cemetery—he took the English name of Rev. William O. Rogers. Tašinasusbecawiŋ, known familiarly just as Susbe, took the English name of Alice Rogers and is buried here at Pejuhutazizi under that name.

This photo postcard was taken in the summer of 1910, when Eunice was still pregnant with Cerisse. Eunice sent it to her mother, Taśinasusbecawiŋ, just a week after she gave birth. In the message on the back, written in Dakota, Eunice sends greetings and shares that she and the baby are fine. Top row, left to right: Fred, Eunice, Taśinasusbecawiŋ (Alice Rogers), William O. Rogers (the Presbyterian minister Susbe married in 1904); bottom row: Evelyn, Estella, Harriet.

Wicaṭe

Pejihutazizi, Granite Falls, Minn. Nakaha Oct. 26 icuŋhaŋ ded wakaŋka waŋ ṭe. He Mrs. Alice Rogers ee qa cajeḣce kiŋ Taśina susbecawiŋ eciyapi. Isaŋyati oyate owasiŋ sdodyapi qa nakuŋ Isaŋyati ehna tawotakuye ota. Oct, 28 ed hapi qa Rev. Henry St. Clair, Caŋśayapi etaŋhaŋ he ehake yuha wacekiyapi owasiŋ yuśtaŋ qa nina taŋyaŋ ouŋkiyapi. Ṭe kiŋ takojakpaku zaptaŋ qa owasiŋ ed oŋpi qeaś waŋna oaśidya eḣpewicaye. —Fred Pearsall

Grandpa Fred submitted this obituary for Taśinasusbecawiŋ to the *Iapi Oaye,* which published it in November 1927. Rev. Henry Whipple St. Clair, the first Dakota to be ordained as an Episcopal priest, performed the service.

Legacy

In regards to names, your grandmother's name was Tašinasusbecawiŋ, but in common speech people always called her Susbe. On the roll at Sisseton Agency, she is Alice Amos, according to your grandfather's name, Joseph Amos. Her first husband took the English name Donnelly. I do not know why, and his son that died in Brown Earth was called Guy Donnelly.

Your great-grandparents, Owakeyaduta and Kata, both had allotments at Sisseton out of the tribal land, but they were both sold long ago, as there were other heirs who wanted to sell. Through your mother, you girls received a share of money from that land, but of course, it was added to other money of ours at the agency and was all in one fund—so, of course, you did not know which money was which.

The older lady, Kata, had her allotment about ten miles northwest of the town of Sisseton, and I never knew where Owakeyaduta's land lay. But I have seen the old lady's land, and it was all level prairie and could all be plowed.

Owakeyaduta and Kata had two children, Joseph and David—your grandfather and Zilla's father up in Ascension. Then they broke up, and the old man married a woman by the name of Wakaŋhdimazawiŋ. Their children were Nancy's mother, Tuŋkaŋwaśtewiŋ, and Makatwaśtewiŋ, Charley Amos's mother. She is buried here up on the hill in the cemetery. Wakaŋhdimazawiŋ died before the allotments were made, so she had no land. There was also another girl, Eliza, who was married to a LeBlanc, but they both died young and had no children. He was a brother of Nancy's father.

Susbe had eight children, but your mother was the only one to survive. So, you can see that you girls are the sole survivors in the family.

PART 4. A STORY OF BELONGING

Utuhu Caŋ Cistiŋna / Teresa Peterson

I imagine if I were asked today for a rendition of a tree, my drawing would look much different from the one I drew twenty years ago. It would be an oak tree, of course. Its trunk would be girthy with thick, rough bark and a story nestled within each crevice. My tree, weighty with so many stories, would be carrying those drawn from my own memories as well as stories that fill former gaps with understanding and knowing. Some of the story crevices run deep, hidden beneath the cool, damp earth, carrying language, history, and places of lives long ago lived. Some of these fissures connect to roots, and more roots meander and tangle with old story. These stories settled deep in the earth—that makes this oak strong and unwavering. They allow this oak's branches to stretch across the vast blue sky, exchanging story with those willing to listen and tell their own. The oak's heart roots breathe in the storyteller's words, and upon exhale the ancient soils shift to make way to travel yet deeper. These are the stories that provide the roots of belonging.

For much of my life, I felt that I did not quite belong in the white world and was missing so much of the Dakota way of life. I have wondered what was worse: to be invisible, or to be reminded you don't belong. How do we reconcile this gap?

We do it through story. Stories connect. Some stories in this collection, as well as those I have researched, provide me with truth and increased understanding, tying the past to the stories I have been told or have told myself. They have nurtured my own humanity, expanding a diverse way of seeing and being in the world. Stories bring me to myself, showing me how I belong.

And I have my own stories to prove it—stories of belonging, stories of values and traditions, and stories of place.

• • • •

One summer afternoon in 2013, as I was sitting on the couch with the little book of my great-grandfather's stories resting on my lap, tears began running down my face.

"What's wrong?" Jay asked with a bit of panic.

"I don't know. I'm just reading my grandmother's story again."

It took me a few days to figure out why I was so upset.

My friend Sharon, who was living in Michigan at the time, had been thinking of coming home. I had been encouraging her to come back to Upper Sioux. She had been researching her family history and became interested in the language. "I've had visitors coming, too. I think it's a sign," she shared with me. We both knew what she meant.

"Come home, then," I pleaded. "I have a job for you—program director at Dakota Wicohaŋ."

Sharon had been divorced for some time and no longer wanted to carry a name that didn't belong to her. Contemplating what name to change to, she landed on Pazi, the name of her great-great-grandfather. It translates as Yellow Head.

I was thinking about this when suddenly, with a rush of blood to my face and adrenaline in my chest, my mind finally understood what my body recognized. It was in Grandpa Fred's book:

> They broke up their home near Ascension where their land was located and came to Granite Falls, Minnesota, in 1897. They stayed here with some of their relatives. It was Pazi and his wife, Itate, that they stayed with, as they had no home of their own here.

In offering Sharon a means to come home, I was able to return an act of goodwill, just as her family—Pazi and Itate—had offered their home to my great-great-grandparents, Susbe and Hotoŋtoŋna. Grandpa's story moved my spirit before my brain had time to make sense of it all.

• • • •

I think about the journey of my great-great-grandma Susbe: the loss of her homeland, the breakup of her people—my people—and her courage and bravery while fleeing north to Canada. She literally dodged bullets as she ran for ammunition.

I mull this story over and over. When I was that age, I was facing the cruel teasing of school bullies, and I wanted to shrivel up, be invisible.

She continued to have loss and tragedy throughout her life. She lost three husbands, and of her eight children, only one, Wakaŋtiomani-wiŋ, survived. That daughter, my great-grandmother, lived just long enough to bring five daughters into the world. The last one, Wihake, my grandma Genevieve, had eight surviving children of her own, including my own mother, Psipsicadaŋwiciyaŋna. These stories have given me a precious gift. I am not here by chance. I descend from a long line of strong, resilient wiŋyaŋ. These are the roots of belonging that I have been searching for all my life.

• • • •

Grandma seemed to always look for the positive in situations. She really was a happy and contented person. She led from this value of wobdi-heiciya or wihaha, a positive outlook on life, in spite of the hardships she endured: boarding school, living through the Depression, losing children. I can still hear her greeting—"Well, Terri, it's good to see you"—and feel her unfailing hospitality. My mom has inherited this same perspective and way of being. No matter the situation, she will look for that silver lining in things. I have often been told to take my rose-colored glasses off—that I might be too naive. Maybe so. But I think I prefer to keep them on.

When Grandma was teaching me the Dakota language, she was also passing on traditions. She taught me how to make fry bread, how to dry corn for waskuya, and how to make plum jelly. When I asked how to best remove the pits, she said, "After it cools some, you just feel for them." You can follow Sure-Jell's directions, add pectin, and have firm jelly, or you can skip it, along with reducing the amount of sugar, to get the tart, soft spread that my grandma and I prefer. Today I make fry bread, dry corn, and gather wild plums around late summer, just as my grandma did. Memories of Grandma travel down to my floured hands as I consider which part of my body carries 25 percent of Kuŋśi. Perhaps it is my two arms, as I am certain my stocky legs came from Grandma Meta on my German side. For it is my two arms that gather vegetables and fruits from my garden and my two hands that chop, mix, and prepare meals for friends and family. And it is my two arms that wrap around my three sons as I silently pray that no matter how far they travel, they will always want to come home. That is how some traditions are. They have a way of summoning memories and stories past, reconnecting to grandmothers and even ancestors long gone.

• • • •

When I was a teenager, Grandpa gave me and my two cousins Dakota names. Wahca Ska Wiŋ, White Flower Woman, is the oldest. Then me, Utuhu Caŋ Cistiŋna, Little Oak Tree. And then the youngest, Wakaŋ Tio Mani Wiŋ, Spirit Walking in the House, who carries our great-grandmother's name. We danced around the circle during the honor song, proud to carry these names. Much later, I came to understand the significance of my name. I am the shortest of us three girls. Grandma told me that Grandpa thought growing up on a farm would make me strong, like the oak trees that filled the front hillside of his place. Once, after I mentioned the meaning behind my name, someone said, "You know, the oak tree takes a long time to mature." Ouch—that stung. Today, however, I don't mind that it took me this long to become the mighty, sturdy oak and am grateful for the stories that fortify me.

The tradition of Dakota name giving continues in our family. My father-in-law gave my oldest, Caske, his name, Uŋśiiciya Mani, He Walks with Humility. He shared that the men he admired most in his life were those that demonstrated humility. Dekśi Super gave the other two boys their names. Hepaŋna's is Ḣtanipi, meaning He Is a Good Worker, and Hepi's is Wicaka, He Speaks the Truth. I have often wondered—do we learn to live up to our Dakota names, or does the spirit whisper the future in a dreaming moment of the name giver? I would like to believe it is a bit of both.

• • • •

I visited Pine Island, the birthplace of my great-great-grandmother, in 2014. In earlier days, it was called Wazu Wita, Island of Pines. A friendly man at the county historical society graciously showed me the place on the hill where many white pines once stood, providing its original place name. I scanned the space and imagined how it might have looked when Susbe was born. He also shared a book, the *History of Goodhue County*. As I read through the history, I came to understand why the space had been a sanctuary for Dakota: it had abundant food sources and was protected during harsh winters. But this history was written in a voice and to an audience that did not include me. It documented the first white child born at Pine Island as Martha Cron. I wish it to be known that Wazu Wita—the Island of Pines—is where Tašinasusbecawiŋ and her twin were born.

• • • •

Some years ago Jay and I moved our family from town to the bluff of the Mni Sota River valley. Our seven acres was once homesteaded by white settlers, easily traced through our land title. Before that, it was treaty land, part of the northern end of the Mdewakaŋtoŋwaŋ reservation, and before that, all Dakota homeland. Today, it is situated in Swedes Forest Township, where we are now the only Dakota inhabitants. Through research and neighborhood stories, I know that the land directly below our hill was once a Dakota campsite. I can envision a camp nestled within the hidden valley, with its creek fed by a year-round natural spring, surrounded by vast prairie. I can imagine temporary Dakota dwellings as our relatives traveled among the various bands and villages. I reflect on this as I walk the deer trails and listen for story and the creek water running nearby. We know we are meant to be here and are grateful for the serendipity of events that led us to move to this space we call home.

• • • •

Stories throughout this collection have brought me deep connections and a stronger sense of belonging. This is now my story of reclaiming, replacing my struggles of belonging, and filling in the cracks and holes of my own story. I recognize that reclaimed stories are the ones our spirit knows. But perhaps we were told a different story, a master narrative that deceives and seeps into our beings as we grow into adults. For as I understand story now, there is no dichotomy, there is no struggle— only a remembering to reclaim our truth, our voice, our stories, that which makes our beings whole again.

This book has taken me close to twenty years to complete, as I have been on a healing journey. I hope that you as the reader reclaim *your* stories of values and traditions, stories of place, stories that entertain, and those that reconcile and make things right. Thomas King writes, "The truth about stories is that that's all we are." I once read that you can tell the state of a society or community by the stories that are told.

Teresa Peterson, 2021. Photo by
Ne-Dah-Ness Greene

What does it say about our society when there is only one story of our collective history that is widely told, shared, or printed? What if we all reclaimed our stories, took the time to share them, listened deeply to others for understanding, and shared and validated these stories in our education systems? If we all reclaim our stories, we will begin to eliminate the disparaging narratives that cause invisibility, harm, and alienation. I hope that the storytellers in this collection provoke the storyteller in you. Share your story.

Waŋna wayake kiŋ sdodwaye—now I know the truth. These roots have extended across time, through the veins of our family tree carrying my grandmothers' strength, courage, and resilience. Now a part of me, this strength, courage, and resilience shall continue on and on to my children and grandchildren. It is this truth that my ancestors whispered in the predawn hours to my grandpa, revealing my Dakota name—my spirit name, Utuhu Caŋ Cistiŋna. Little Oak Tree. This nocturnal revelation ushering in a knowing so that I would come to understand: I belong. I belong.

ACKNOWLEDGMENTS

Wopida taŋka eciciyapi!

There are so many I owe a debt of gratitude for making this overdue project a reality. Many thanks to: Ann Regan, for her clever cajoling, dedication, and patience; Darlene St. Clair, for her writing retreat space; my Native Women's Writing Group, especially Gabrielle Tateyuskanskan, who asked those tough questions; the late Francis Country, for those pivotal words; Diane Wilson, for brainstorming, providing feedback, and cheering me on; Tom Peacock, Heather Peters, Nora Murphy, and Mary Peters, for review, feedback, and encouragement; Bruce White for early archival documents; Jay, my rock and partner; Ma, who kept me connected to place and relatives. And to Cerisse—I hope you can see this from the spirit world. Waŋna abdustan!

Utuhu Cistiŋna Wiŋ, Teresa Peterson

I wish to thank my relative Eric Olson and the many others who have provided me with information on our family's genealogy over the last thirty years—you know who you are! Also Bruce White for fact-checking support. I am especially grateful to all those elders of my youth who shared their stories with me. Wopida!

Wašicuŋhdinażiŋ, Walter LaBatte Jr. de miye do.

NOTES ON EDITING AND ORTHOGRAPHY

A few notes to consider as you read this book:

Honoring Authenticity. We share stories as told and heard from Peju-hutazizi, yet we do not necessarily represent the whole of Pejuhutazizi, nor the Dakota Oyate, nor Native people in general. Additionally,

> The stories told by Waŋbdiska—Grandpa Fred—are tran-scribed from the versions published by my Aunt Cerisse In-gebritson (see full citation in Notes to Sidebars). The original writings are in the possession of Walter LaBatte Jr.
>
> Almost every story in Cerisse's book is included. We have cor-rected typos, regularized spellings of names, applied diacritical marks in the spellings of Dakota words and names, inserted missing words, corrected an error or two, and merged two tellings of the buffalo hunt. Some words that Grandpa Fred uses are unfamiliar or outdated (e.g., Chippeways, half-breed); we have retained them to maintain his authentic voice.
>
> The spelling of individual names is a matter of individual pref-erence: some people prefer having the parts of the name written as individual words, others prefer them written as one word. We have attempted to honor each individual's preference when it is known. When it is not known, we have generally spelled them as a single word.

Honoring Multiple Stories. Someone may share another story or ver-sion that differs from what is told here. This is not a contradiction but another perspective or experience. All are valid.

Honoring Place. There are multiple Dakota orthographies, and the one used in this book is the one most often used at Pejuhutazizi. It is the version used in *A Dakota-English Dictionary* created in the 1840s by the missionaries Stephen R. Riggs and Thomas Williamson. Additionally,

> The Dakota alphabet includes sounds that are not found in English. For example, the Dakota letter ḣ that is used in waḣpopa and ḣanteśadaŋ is a guttural sound. The nasal ŋ is similar to the n sound in the English word ink. Accents typically fall on the second syllable. A video created by Dakota Wicoḣaŋ giving pronunciations of the letters in the Dakota alphabet is available at https://tinyurl.com/DWDakotaAlphabet.

> There are multiple spellings of pejuhuta and Pejuhutazizi that differ from Riggs and Williamson's; they spell the words peźihuta and Peźihutazi.

Honoring Dakota Storytelling. This is a book of stories—not a text for learning or teaching Dakota language.

FAMILY TREE

··

The family tree on the following three pages shows the relationships among many of the people discussed in this book's stories. We include names and dates as we have been able to find them.

Peterson/LaBatte Families

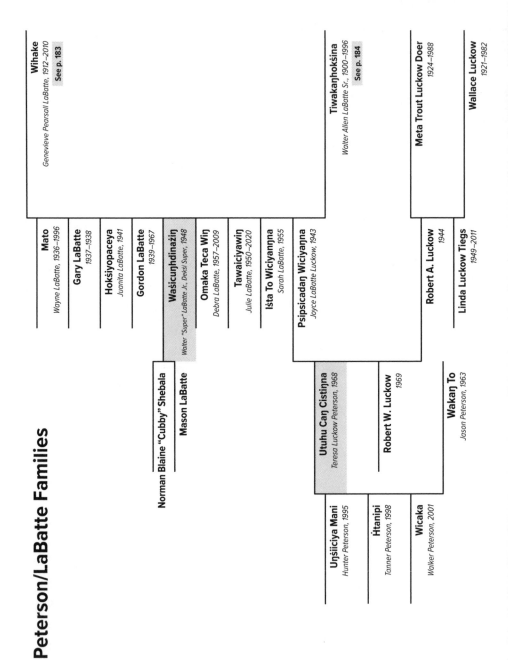

Wihake
Genevieve Pearsall LaBatte, 1912–2010
See p. 183

Mato
Wayne LaBatte, 1936–1996

Gary LaBatte
1937–1938

Hoksíyopaceya
Juanita LaBatte, 1941

Gordon LaBatte
1939–1967

Wašicuŋhdinaziŋ
Walter "Super" LaBatte Jr., Deksi Super, 1948

Omaka Teca Wiŋ
Debra LaBatte, 1957–2009

Tawaiciyawiŋ
Julie LaBatte, 1950–2020

Ista To Wiciyaŋna
Sarah LaBatte, 1955

Psipsicadaŋ Wiciyaŋna
Joyce LaBatte Luckow, 1943

Norman Blaine "Cubby" Shebala

Mason LaBatte

Tiwakaŋhoksina
Walter Allen LaBatte Sr., 1900–1996
See p. 184

Meta Trout Luckow Doer
1924–1988

Robert A. Luckow
1944

Linda Luckow Tiegs
1949–2011

Wallace Luckow
1921–1982

Utuhu Caŋ Cistiŋna
Teresa Luckow Peterson, 1968

Robert W. Luckow
1969

Wakaŋ To
Jason Peterson, 1963

Uŋšiiciya Mani
Hunter Peterson, 1995

Ḣtaniipi
Tanner Peterson, 1998

Wicaka
Walker Peterson, 2001

Amos/Pearsall Families

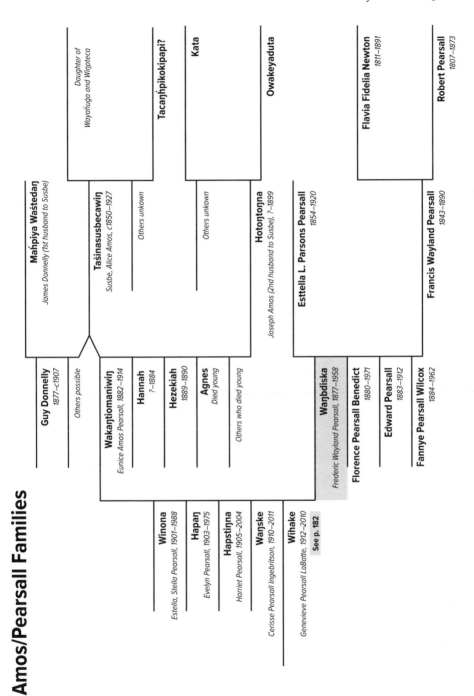

Maĥpiya Waśtedaŋ
James Donnelly (1st husband to Susbe)

Daughter of
Wayahuga and Wiŋpteca

Taśinasusbecawiŋ
Susbe, Alice Amos, c1850–1927

Tacaŋĥpikokipapi?

Others unkown

Kata

Others unkown

Hotoŋtoŋna
Joseph Amos (2nd husband to Susbe), ?–1899

Owakeyaduta

Guy Donnelly
1877–c1907

Others possible

Wakaŋtiomaniwiŋ
Eunice Amos Pearsall, 1882–1914

Hannah
?–1884

Hezekiah
1889–1890

Agnes
Died young

Others who died young

Esttella L. Parsons Pearsall
1854–1920

Flavia Fidelia Newton
1811–1891

Francis Wayland Pearsall
1843–1890

Robert Pearsall
1807–1873

Waŋbdiska
Frederic Wayland Pearsall, 1877–1958

Florence Pearsall Benedict
1880–1971

Edward Pearsall
1883–1912

Fannye Pearsall Wilcox
1884–1962

Winona
Estella, Stella Pearsall, 1901–1988

Hapaŋ
Evelyn Pearsall, 1903–1975

Hapstiŋna
Harriet Pearsall, 1905–2004

Waŋske
Cerisse Pearsall Ingebritson, 1910–2011

Wihake
Genevieve Pearsall LaBatte, 1912–2010

See p. 182

Renville/LaBatte Families

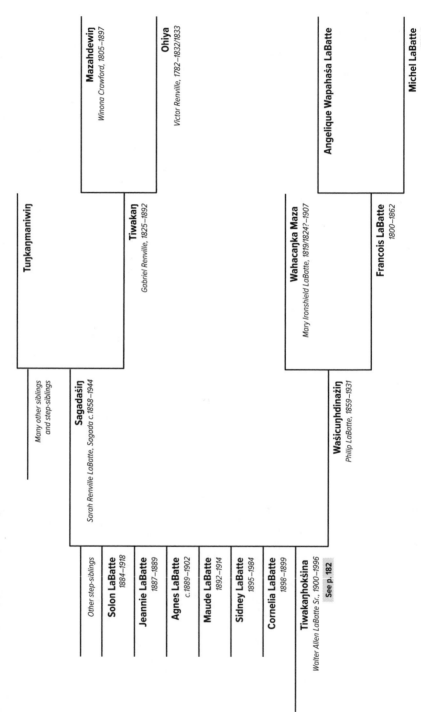

Tuŋkaŋmaniwiŋ

Mazahdewiŋ
Winona Crawford, 1805–1897

Tiwakaŋ
Gabriel Renville, 1825–1892

Ohiya
Victor Renville, 1782–1832/1833

Many other siblings
and step-siblings

Sagadasiŋ
Sarah Renville LaBatte, Sagada c. 1858–1944

Other step-siblings

Solon LaBatte
1884–1918

Jeannie LaBatte
1887–1889

Agnes LaBatte
c. 1889–1902

Maude LaBatte
1892–1914

Sidney LaBatte
1895–1984

Cornelia LaBatte
1898–1899

Tiwakaŋhokšina
Walter Allen LaBatte Sr., 1900–1996

See p. 182

Wašicuŋhdinaziŋ
Philip LaBatte, 1859–1931

Wahacaŋka Maza
Mary Ironshield LaBatte, 1819/1824?–1907

Francois LaBatte
1800–1862

Angelique Wapahaša LaBatte

Michel LaBatte
1781–?

NOTES TO SIDEBARS

....

Utuhu Caŋ Cistiŋna / Teresa Peterson

Some of the information provided in sidebars relates specifically to our family's history, and the sources are in our possession. These include probate records for Susbe and Walter LaBatte Sr.; Fred Pearsall's memorial service program; letters from and interviews with Cerisse Pearsall Ingebritson; the Pearsall family Bible (in another family member's possession); and miscellaneous other papers. We also used various genealogical websites.

My own thoughts on story and belonging are summarized in my dissertation, "Exploring a Cultural Intervention's Influence on Sense of Belonging: Bringing Dakota Story into 6th and 10th Grade Social Studies Classrooms," DEd, University of Minnesota, 2015, which is available at the University of Minnesota Digital Conservancy, https://hdl .handle.net/11299/175299.

In addition, these sources have provided essential background information for this work:

Iapi Oaye. Minnesota Digital Library Hub, Minnesota Historical Society.

LaBatte, Walter [Sr]. Oral History Interview by Vijay Gupta, 1968. American Indian Research Project, South Dakota Oral History Center. Available at https://cdm17102.contentdm.oclc.org/digital/ collection/sdohc/id/118.

Narvestad, Carl and Amy. *A History of Yellow Medicine County, Minnesota, 1872–1972.* Granite Falls, MN: Yellow Medicine County Historical Society, 1972.

Pearsall, Fred. *Short Stories and History of Dakota People.* [Phoenix, AZ]: Cerisse Ingebritson, 1983.

Renville, Gabriel. "A Sioux Narrative of the Outbreak in 1862, and of Sibley's Expedition in 1863." Trans. Thomas A. Robertson. *Collections of the Minnesota Historical Society* 10 (1905): 596–618. The original Dakota text is in the Joseph R. and Samuel J. Brown and family papers, 1826–1956, at the Minnesota Historical Society.

Rogers, Elwin E. *For God & Land: Brown Earth, a Dakota Indian Community, 1876–1892*. Sioux Falls, SD: Pine Hill Press, 2002. This book contains appendixes that list those who lived at Brown Earth.

Westerman, Gwen, and Bruce White. *Mni Sota Makoce: The Land of the Dakota*. St. Paul: MNHS Press, 2012.

p. 32, Dakota–US War: Many books have been published about this war, almost all of them from the whites' point of view. Perhaps the most useful summary is in Mary Lethert Wingerd, *North Country: The Making of Minnesota* (Minneapolis: University of Minnesota Press, 2010), 301–45.

p. 33, Hazelwood Republic: Westerman and White, *Mni Sota Makoce,* 120; Wingerd, *North Country,* 273.

p. 34, Camp Release: Wingerd, *North Country,* 312–34; Carol Chomsky, "The United States–Dakota War Trials: A Study in Military Injustice," *Stanford Law Review* 43 (November 1990): 40.

p. 39, Flandreau Indian School: A history of the school is provided on the website of the Flandreau Indian School Chaplaincy Program, www.fischaplaincy.com/school-history.

p. 50, *Iapi Oaye*: This newspaper is available online through the Minnesota Digital Newspaper Hub, https://www.mnhs.org/newspapers/hub/word-carrier, which includes a brief overview of the publishing history.

p. 53, Waśicuŋ's trial: John Isch, *The Dakota Trials: The 1862–1864 Military Commission Trials* (New Ulm, MN: Brown County Historical Society), 338–39.

p. 55, Morris Industrial School: Wilbert H. Ahern, "Indian Education and Bureaucracy: The School at Morris, 1887–1909," *Minnesota History* 49, no. 3 (Fall 1984): 82–98.

p. 65, Tiwakaŋ's memories: Renville, "A Sioux Narrative of the Outbreak in 1862, and of Sibley's Expedition in 1863."

p. 76, Oceti Śakowiŋ and diaspora: Westerman and White, *Mni Sota Makoce,* 22; Dakota Removal Act: Congressional Act of March 3, 1863, ch. 119, 12 Stat. 819.

p. 86, White Earth Celebration and Powwow: Frances Densmore, "An Ojibwa Council Fire," *Indian School Journal* (December 1906): 21, quoted in Marcia G. Anderson, *A Bag Worth a Pony: The Art of the Ojibwe Bandolier Bag* (St. Paul: MNHS Press, 2017), 186–90.

p. 101, riverboat attack: Red Blanket's story is in Joseph Henry Taylor, *Sketches of Frontier and Indian Life on the Upper Missouri and Great Plains* (Bismarck: [The Author], 1897), 216–22. For more on this event, see Hiram Martin Chittenden, *History of Early Steamboat Navigation on the Missouri River, Volume II: Life and Adventures of Joseph La Barge* (New York: Francis P. Harper, 1903), 278; Clement Augustus Lounsberry, *Early History of North Dakota: Essential Outlines of American History* (Washington, DC: Liberty Press, 1919), 292; Micheal Clodfelter, *The Dakota War: The United States Army Versus the Sioux, 1862–1865* (Jefferson, NC: McFarland, 1998), 54–57.

p. 103, Nasuna Taŋka: Roberta Estes, "Chief Big Head, Standing Rock, Dakota Territory," posted September 12, 2014, at https://nativeheritageproject.com.

p. 105, Lazarus Skyman: This census is in Frederic M. Pearsall to F. F. Mann, December 26, 1918, Correspondence, Box 16, Censuses, Pipestone Indian School, Minnesota, 1895–1952, Record Group 75, National Archives at Kansas City.

p. 117, 1837 treaty: Westerman and White, *Mni Sota Makoce,* 161.

p. 119, 1851 treaty: Westerman and White, *Mni Sota Makoce,* 182.

p. 120, Iŋkpaduta: Peggy Rodina Larson, "A New Look at the Elusive Inkpaduta," *Minnesota History* 48, no. 1 (Spring 1982): 24–35.

p. 124, Battle of Greasy Grass: Hundreds of books have been written about this battle. For a summary, see Jennifer Davis, "The Battle of Greasy Grass," In Custodia Legis blog, Law Librarians of Congress, June 25, 2020, https://blogs.loc.gov/law/2020/06/the-battle-of-greasy-grass/.

p. 125, Ohiyesa: Katherine Beane, "Woyakapi Kin Ahdipi 'Bringing the Story Home': A History Within the Wakpa Ipaksan Dakota Oyate," PhD diss., University of Minnesota, 2014.

p. 126, termination: Donald L. Fixico, *Termination and Relocation: Federal Indian Policy, 1945–1960* (Albuquerque: University of New Mexico Press, 1990).

p. 128, Sonosky: Wolfgang Saxon, "Marvin J. Sonosky, 88, Lawyer
Who Championed Indian Cause," *New York Times,* July 21, 1997.

p. 142, Dakota villages: Westerman and White, *Mni Sota Makoce,* 192.

p. 143, names: Fred Pearsall, "Sioux Geographic Names, April 24,
1912," MNHS Collections.

p. 145 and 146, Riggs: Stephen Return Riggs, *A Dakota-English
Dictionary* (1890; repr., St. Paul: MNHS Press, 1992).

p. 149, Pillager attack: William W. Warren, *History of the Ojibway
People,* ed. Theresa Schenck (St. Paul: MNHS Press, 2009),
280–81.

p. 150, Brown and Robertson: Jane Lamm Carroll, *Daybreak Woman:
An Anglo-Dakota Life* (St. Paul: MNHS Press, 2020), 60, 85, 100.

p. 156, Métis hunters: Brenda Macdougall and Nicole St. Onge,
"Rooted in Mobility: Metis Buffalo Hunting Brigades," *Manitoba
History* 71 (Winter 2013): 21–32.

p. 158, Hudson's Bay Company: For a Native perspective on the HBC,
see *The Other Side of the Ledger: An Indian View of the Hudson's
Bay Company,* available at http://www.nfb.ca/film/other_side_
of_the_ledger/. This 1972 film was codirected by Martin Defalco
and Willie Dunn. Dunn was a member of an all-Indigenous
production unit established in 1968 at the National Film Board
of Canada.

p. 161, Flandreau: Roy W. Meyer, *History of the Santee Sioux: United
States Indian Policy on Trial* (Lincoln: University of Nebraska
Press, 1967), 242–57, 340.

p. 163, Sauk and Meskwaki: Westerman and White, *Mni Sota Makoce,*
68, 154.

p. 165, Brown Earth and Dawes Act: Meyer, *History of the Santee
Sioux,* 215, 350; Rose Stremlau, "'To Domesticate and Civilize Wild
Indians': Allotment and the Campaign to Reform Indian Families,
1875–1887," *Journal of Family History* 30, no. 3 (July 2005): 265–86.

p. 168, obituary: The *Granite Falls Tribune* also published an obituary
on November 2, 1927.

GLOSSARY

....

This glossary does not include words that appear once and are translated in the text; we also do not include people's names or most place names, which often have multiple translations.

ate—father.
Bde Caŋ—Wood Lake.
Bdehdakiŋyaŋ—Lake Traverse.
canḣdoḣu apemadaska—flat weed; referring to the broadleaf plantain.
caŋ—wood.
caŋkuoiyute—road measure, mile.
caŋpa—chokecherries.
caŋśaśa—red willow.
Caŋśaśa Wakpadaŋ—Red Willow Creek.
Caŋśayapi—where they paint the trees red; the name of the Lower Sioux Indian Community.
Caske—first-born son.
caże—name.
cici—slang word for monster.   .
Dakota—friend or ally; also, the easternmost of the seven bands of the Oceti Śakowiŋ, the people sometimes called the Sioux.
Dakota ia—in Dakota speech or language, or the command, "Speak Dakota."
Dakota Wicohaŋ—Dakota Way of Life.
Damakota—I am Dakota.
dekśi—uncle.
emakiyapi ye/do—they call me (female/male).
eyapaha—camp crier.
haŋ—female greeting or affirmative, yes.
Hapaŋ—second-born daughter.
Hapstiŋna—third-born daughter.

hau—male greeting or affirmative, yes.

Hepaŋ, Hepaŋna—second-born boy, little second-born boy.

Hepi—third-born boy.

Ho hecetu—yes, it is so; that's the way it is.

Ho hecetu mitakuyapi. Hau de miye do Wašicuŋhdinaži̇ŋ emakiyapi do.—Yes, this is so, my relatives. This is me. I'm called Wasicunhdinazi.

hokšina, hokšidaŋ—little boy.

hotaiŋ—elk whistle.

Hotaŋke—Big Voices, the Dakota word for Ho-Chunk (Winnebago).

huhu—cry of alarm.

huŋka—adopted.

Ḣahatoŋwaŋ—Dwellers by the Falls, the Dakota word for Ojibwe; Chippewa and Chippeway are earlier spellings.

Ḣe Sapa—Black Hills.

Ḣeipa—one of the districts on the Sisseton Reservation, near Veblen, South Dakota; the name means the top of a hill, especially the start of the Coteau des Prairies.

ḣeku—below the hill.

Ḣtayetu aomahaŋzi, Taku waŋ awacaŋmi—The first lines of the Presbyterian hymn referred to as the Evening Song, which continues, "Tona mitokam iyaye, Hena weksuya ece," and loosely translates as, "The evening shades me / I'm in the shade of the night, I'm thinking of that one. How many have gone before me, those I remember."

icazo—to buy on credit.

icepaŋši—female cousin, in female speech.

Ihaŋktonwaŋna—Yanktonnai, Little Dwellers at the End; one of the Seven Council Fires of the Oceti Šakowiŋ.

Ihaŋktoŋwaŋ —Yankton, Dwellers at the End; one of the Seven Council Fires of the Oceti Šakowiŋ.

ina—mother.

inipi, initipi—sweat, sweat lodge.

Isaŋati—Eastern band of Dakota, Dwellers by the Knife (River); sometimes spelled Isanyati or Isaŋti. They are known in English as the Isanti or Santee.

Iyakaptapi—refers to the Ascension Church near Big Coulee, South Dakota; translates as they go up or ascend.

kaḣmiŋ—bend in a river.

koda/kola—friend, ally (Dakota/Lakota).

kohdi—flint corn.

kuŋśi—grandmother.

Lakota—see Titoŋwaŋ.

maka—mother earth, land.

Maka Saŋ—Gray Earth.

makaiyutapi—earth measure, mile.

mato—bear.

Maya Saŋ—Grey Cliff.

Mdewakaŋtoŋwaŋ, Bdewakaŋtoŋwaŋ—Mdewakanton, Bdewakanton, Dwellers of the Spirit Lake; one of the Seven Council Fires of the Oceti Śakowiŋ.

miniheca—hard worker, being active.

mitakuye, mitakuyapi—my relative, my relatives.

mitakuye owasiŋ—All my relations; includes all things in the natural world, animals, plants, rocks, and more.

Mni Sota—refers to the land of cloudy waters; the source of the name for Minnesota.

Mni Sota Wakpa—Minnesota River.

naceca—probably.

Nakota—Refers to the Ihaŋktonwaŋ and Ihaŋktonwaŋna.

nina—very.

odowaŋ, odowaŋpi—song, songs.

ohaŋśica—stingy.

ohaŋwaśte—generosity.

okodakiciye—joint meeting of allies; in a religious context, a mission meeting.

oyate—nation.

paśdayapi—literally, they make it bald; refers to soup made with lyed corn.

Pejuhutazizi, Pejuhutazizi K'api—yellow medicine, where they dig the yellow medicine; the name of the Upper Sioux Indian Community.

pejuta—medicine.

Śakpe—Shakopee Mdewakantonwan reservation.

sececa, secece—it seems.

śica—bad.

Sicaŋǧu—Burnt Thigh band of Lakota.

śiceca—child.

Sisitoŋwaŋ—Sisseton, Dwellers of the Fishing Grounds; one of the Seven Council Fires of the Oceti Śakowiŋ.

śtuŋka—unripe.

śuŋka—dog.

tahaŋ—brother-in-law, in male speech.

tahaŋśi—male cousin, in male speech.

tataŋka—buffalo.

tawaciŋ waśte—good will, good mind, good disposition.

tiośpaye—those who cook together; generally, extended family.

tipsiŋna—prairie turnip.

Titoŋwaŋ—Titonwan, Lakota, Dwellers of the Prairie; one of the Seven Council Fires of the Oceti Śakowiŋ.

Tiyotipi—Soldiers' Lodge.

tuŋkaŋśidaŋ/tuŋkaŋśina/tuŋkaŋśila—grandfather (Dakota/Nakota/Lakota).

Uŋktomi—spider; the Dakota trickster.

wacipi—they dance, a dance (powwow).

wahiŋkte—elk antler scraper.

Waȟpekute—Wahpekute, Shooters among the Leaves; one of the Seven Council Fires of the Oceti Śakowiŋ.

Waȟpetoŋ, Waȟpetoŋwaŋ—Wahpeton, Dwellers among the Leaves; one of the Seven Council Fires of the Oceti Śakowiŋ.

Wakaŋtaŋka—great spirit, great mystery.

wakpa—river.

wamnaheza—corn, maize.

Wanske—fourth-born daughter.

waŋna abdustaŋ—I'm done now.

Wapahaśa—red standard or staff; the name of several hereditary Mdewakaŋtoŋwaŋ leaders; it has been anglicized as Wabasha.

waśicuŋ—white man; *diminutive* waśicuŋna.

waskuya—sweet corn.

waśte—good.

waśtuŋkala—dried sweet corn (Lakota).

waziya—Santa, old man winter, north.

wetu—spring.

wica—man.
wicašta—man.
wicaṭe—death announcement (sometimes spelled wicaṭa).
wiŋyaŋ—woman.
wojapi—pudding.
wopida taŋka, wopida—great thanks, gratitude.

ABOUT THE AUTHORS

Teresa Peterson is a planner, evaluator, gardener, and writer. She is Sisseton-Wahpeton Dakota and a member of the Upper Sioux Community.

Walter LaBatte Jr. is an artist who tans hides, makes drums, beads moccasins, and prepares pasdayapi. He is Sisseton-Wahpeton Dakota and a member of the Upper Sioux Community.

Voices from Pejuhutazizi has been typeset in Minion, a typeface designed by Robert Slimbach. It is inspired by late Renaissance-era type and designed for body text in a classic style.

Book design by Wendy Holdman